SHEPHERD'S PIE

SHEPHERD'S PIE

FAMILY BUSINESS, RECESSION & RECOVERY

THE REAL STORY

GEORGE MORDAUNT

MERCIER PRESS
Irish Publisher – Irish Story

MERCIER PRESS

Cork

www.mercierpress.ie

© George Mordaunt, 2011

© Foreword: Fergus Finlay, 2011

ISBN: 978 1 85635 844 6

10 9 8 7 6 5 4 3 2 1

A CIP record for this title is available from the British Library

Printed and bound in the EU.

Contents

To Anne, Emily and George –
you are and always will be my reason.
I love you. xxx

Foreword

I first met George Mordaunt a few years ago, when he expressed an interest in our work with disadvantaged children and offered to help by raising a substantial investment for Barnardos. To be honest, I thought at first he was a bit flash – every inch the Celtic Tiger entrepreneur. But he was clearly a totally committed family man and a loving parent, and that reflected itself in the sincerity of his commitment to Barnardos.

When we agreed to 'partner up', George immediately set about introducing an innovative way of linking financial support for a good cause with car sales. The day we launched the scheme (typical George!) he had organised a whirlwind of local publicity and advertising to back it up. Barnardos was heavily profiled, but so was the Mordaunt Group – a real win-win situation.

Throughout the years we've worked together, I've never known anything about George's private struggles, or indeed the demons he was grappling with. So it came as a real shock to sit down and read this book. It is the most searingly honest account I've read anywhere about what it was like to ride the Tiger – and ultimately to be almost devoured by it.

This is a book that deserves to be read by everyone who has lived through the highs and lows of the last fifteen years. It is totally gripping in its honesty, to the point of being painful at times. George might seem pretty brash on the outside, but he is clearly a man only too well aware of his own failings. In that sense, he blames himself as much as anyone else for the cocksureness that almost destroyed him.

But he has a lot of advice to offer in the book. It's advice based on the lessons he knows he should have learned, and it's advice that has made him a lot happier since he stopped trying to be king of the hill. It's advice that is worth following in a lot of walks of life.

It's unusual to finish a book like this – I found it hard to tear myself away from it – and find yourself reflecting that you've also been privy to a warm and decent love story. George's relationship with his parents, and especially with his wife and children, is just that, and it's beautifully written about here.

Now, if I had one bit of advice for the reader of this book, it's this. Stop reading this foreword right now, and get stuck into one of the best books you're ever likely to read about what went wrong in our country and why. Oh, and by the way, how to come out of it all as a better, stronger person.

Fergus Finlay
CEO
Barnardos

Prologue

'Save the sob story. We want our money. If that means taking your family home, we'll do it.'

I was stunned. Couldn't believe what I was hearing. This banker, playing with words, puffing his chest out in a display of ego and bravado, telling me how ruthless he would be with my home, my livelihood, my life. My shocked and fearful reaction was probably nothing new to him, and the more I pleaded and tried to rationalise, the more powerful he became.

Fifteen hours later I lay in bed feeling nauseous and gripped with fear. My home was at stake. This was an assault on my inner sanctum. I was deeply upset, in absolute turmoil. My heart was pounding so hard I could hear it in my chest, my mind actively replaying the scene in the bank's boardroom that morning. My mental health had been under attack for months, but so far I had held it together. To lose that battle now would have devastating effects on my wife and kids, my extended family, my business and employees. People were depending on me. Losing it wasn't an option. I knew that I was emotionally and financially broken and that the family business that I had cherished was on the brink.

My heart was pounding faster, but that feeling had become familiar. These episodes were becoming much more frequent and each one was more intense than the last. I got up and walked to the window. I started talking to myself, trying to calm my racing heartbeat. It wasn't working and I wondered if I should call my wife to tell her that I thought I was having a heart attack and ask her to call an ambulance. But I found that I had absentmindedly wandered into my son's bedroom. I needed to be close to my kids and that was calming me down.

My eight-year-old son lay there sleeping, so innocent and oblivious to everything that was going on in the world. I gazed down at him and thought about another man, my age, who I had known very well. His kids were the same age as mine and he had lost his battle with control and fear one evening. It was a tragedy that affected the entire community, not to mention the trauma for his own family. I couldn't let that happen, but bizarrely I found myself imagining that it had. I sat on the side of my son's bed and imagined my own funeral, with my son and my daughter walking behind a hearse. I wondered whether I was losing my mind but knew I wasn't. I allowed the pain of the image to take hold and then something I wasn't expecting happened. Anger started to emerge from the pit of my stomach. Fury. I screamed to myself – are you going to let those fuckers deprive these children of their father? Are you going to allow them to attack your family and everything that your family has created? Are you going to let them inside the gates of your home or are you going to meet them head on and tell them to fuck off?

Suddenly I realised that that was exactly what I had to do. I wondered how many other people lie awake at night with the same fears? How many people are on the verge of losing everything? I am not alone. Sitting there in my son's bedroom at 3.45 a.m., I could finally think clearly. I was going to have to fight this even harder. Lose the fear and stand up to those bullies in their open-collared shirts and rolled-up sleeves. I would never forgive myself if I didn't. If I managed to hang in there, I would never allow this to happen again, and if I ended up losing everything anyway, I would be proud that I had taken a stand, spoken out and could with hand on heart look my kids in the eye and say that I did everything in my power to save our home and livelihood.

My fight would start back at the office within five hours when I began to actively change my mindset to fight back. A short time later I confronted the bank that had my family home in its sights. I stood behind my desk, picked up the phone and dialled. While staring at a photo sitting on my desk of my wife Anne, my daughter Emily and my son George, I laid down the gauntlet. 'Listen to me very carefully. I refuse to let you or any other bank force my wife and children to walk behind a hearse, so do your worst but don't ever call me again.'

I put the phone down, stood in silence staring at it for

about twenty seconds, then turned to a colleague who was in the room with me and said, 'What's next?'

Chapter 1

Life through the Lens of 1986

Youth is, after all, just a moment, but it is the moment, the spark, that you always carry in your heart.

Raisa Gorbachev

Born to Brian and Bridie Mordaunt in November 1967 in St Joseph's Hospital, Clonmel, I was the second-eldest of four children. I had two sisters, Lizanne and Claire, and one brother, Brian. I was raised in Clonmel and continue to reside there today. Outside of school, life was reasonably ordinary. I had a loving family and I have fond memories of my childhood, notwithstanding my schooldays. My parents were loving, supportive and protective, as well as being relatively well off – we were lucky enough to be able to have a family holiday abroad almost every year.

My schooldays were certainly not the best days of my life. I hated school with a passion. I dreaded going to school and looking back now I still remember just how much. My years at the hands of the Irish educational system proved to be disastrous, to the point where I still feel bitterly let down. To this day I have to control my feelings towards the institution, indeed sometimes even towards teachers themselves. I was schooled at the CBS primary and secondary schools in Kickham Street, Clonmel. I think there must have been an academic ranking system for the classes and I seemed to have been consigned to one of the lower grades. I failed almost every exam that I ever took. In fifth year in secondary school I remember sitting at my desk wondering if I was 'slow'. What makes a fifteen-year-old boy consider that? The answer is that the ranking system had failed me and that failure would go on to make a definite impact on my future business life.

When I was seven years old my primary-school teacher asked me to think of a word that began with the letter G. Given my name, you would think that it would have been no problem for me, but my mind went blank and I couldn't think of anything. As punishment for this, the teacher insisted that I put on a dress and stand at the front of the class where everybody could see me. The rest of the class thought it was hilarious, but I can still feel the hurt and humiliation I suffered that day. Why would somebody do that to a child? Did I irritate her? What was her agenda? Later, the teacher insisted that I keep my mouth shut about this and never tell my parents. She must have known that she had overstepped the mark. Of course, like thousands of kids before me, on the instruction of an authority figure I did exactly what I was told and never said a word.

Some weeks later my best friend at the time told my mother this hilarious story. She was furious and later challenged all parties involved, but for me it was too late. The incident had deprived me of every morsel of self-confidence. In that one moment I was robbed of my education. That was the severity of the impact of that episode. Even today, when I think about it, it angers me and I know irrefutably that the incident not only affected my childhood and education, but also the path I followed in my adult life, because I was branded that day. Branded as stupid, laughable, and as a result I clammed up every time I was asked a question at school. It became habitual. Hence I was perceived as stupid and I believed I was stupid. That is how I was made to feel and it became my status for my entire school career.

By third class I found myself sitting on the knee of a Christian brother as he rolled his hand around the inside of my underwear feeling the cheeks of my bottom. Teachers used violence and terror to control unruly students – window poles used for opening old sash windows, hurleys, leather straps, fists, all were used on various parts of our bodies. I watched pupils fight with teachers, watched kids drink beer at 11 a.m., and saw one boy intentionally break his finger by placing it between the top and bottom part of a writing desk and pound the top up and down until his finger broke, just so that he could get time off school. It was clearly dysfunctional and despite one or two teachers who really tried, the majority didn't seem to give a shit. They did their time and if a kid drifted away, so be it. Did they nurture, develop, breed confidence and encourage us? Far from it. In my opinion, between the sexual, physical and emotional abuse in Irish schools, many kids of that generation were deprived of their right to a decent education, development and encouragement. That generation today runs Ireland Inc. No wonder the country is banjaxed.

School had served only to make me unhappy, to suppress my confidence and talent – and I went to school in the 1980s not the 1930s. As a result of my complete lack of self-belief and self-confidence I found it impossible to find myself a job once I left – further education didn't even occur to me because I firmly believed I was stupid. My father intervened and using his local connections I managed to land a job as a postman after I left school in 1986. I had left school four months before my Leaving Cert, but I would return to sit the exams, which I failed. So my life as a postman began at the age of seventeen.

I thought the job would be easy, but I was wrong. My first day was a 6 a.m. start on a Monday morning in November. I was given a High Nelly bike and 355 letters. I had to cover four housing estates and hundreds of houses in numerical order – almost. They started off 1, 2, 3, 4, 5, 6, 7, 8, 9, 10, then suddenly jumped to 22, 23, 24, 25. No sign of 11 to 21.

I didn't care nor did I look too hard for the missing houses either. Needless to say, I didn't make a very good postman. I was far too preoccupied with my new girlfriend Anne and my career as a DJ on a pirate radio station. The post job was a distraction that I didn't really want, so I hatched a plan to reduce my time on the route. I would re-post the post. I'd collect the post and my bike every morning at 6 a.m. and promptly post it back through the nearest postbox and worry about it tomorrow. When the letters I had re-posted arrived back to my station, I would burn them in my parents' back garden – unbeknownst to them. What an asshole! Anne used to find letters stuffed under the seat of my Ford Fiesta and she would deliver some of them after she finished school.

After six months An Post must have figured out what I was doing because I was fired, although they never actually said why. I went on to have a very short-lived stint as a bread delivery man for a bakery. Again, I simply wanted an easy life so I could concentrate on my girlfriend and being a DJ, but it wasn't to be. Do you know how many types of bread you need to know about in order to sell bread successfully? Too many for me. Seven days later – fired.

There were two great loves in my life at the time. The first was Anne Hickey, who I had met a few weeks before starting my postman's job. I had seen her at a church service that both our schools were attending. She was way too cool for me, but I must have done something right because she agreed to marry me and we tied the knot in 1993 after a seven-year relationship. We are still happily married.

My other great love was radio. From the age of fifteen I had been a presenter on a local pirate radio station. I loved it and was good at it – it was the one job that I was confident I could do and didn't feel stupid at. Radio was where my real passion lay. Yet years later, when new, legal and licensed radio stations were started, I foolishly turned down an opportunity to have a full-time career in radio broadcasting.

In my opinion very few people get to discover what their real passion is, never mind get an opportunity to pursue that passion on a full-time basis and get paid for it. I believe that every parent has a responsibility to try to help each of his or her children to discover their passion. It might not always be possible to cultivate it, but when it is, it must be encouraged. Imagine a world where the working masses went to work to do a job that they were passionate about? What a difference it would make. The following questions apparently test your level of passion for life. You're supposed to choose a level of agreement with each statement, ranking from 'Never' to 'All the time' for 1 to 6 and for question 7 'No sense of direction' to 'Very clear sense of direction'.[1]

1. I am excited about my life and turned on by the things I get to do each day.

---

1   www.thepassiontest.com/offer/ptprofile/

2. Others comment on how happy I am and what fun it is to be around me.

3. I get upset and thrown off track when unexpected situations and circumstances arise.

4. I am very clear about the top five passions in my life, those things that matter most to me.

5. I make decisions based on what will help me live my passions most fully.

6. I spend my days doing things I love, surrounded by people I love.

7. Life is confusing for me. I don't have a clear sense of direction in my life.

It's an interesting test to take and the results might surprise you. I believe that if I had pursued a career in radio I would consistently have had a high score, but I decided on a different path. I chose the family business.

Having been fired from the bakery, it wasn't a huge surprise when my father offered me a job – I had run out of options really and my father had a glittering career in the motor industry. He and my mother Bridie had moved to Tipperary from Wexford in 1961, and my father had started as a parts salesman for a large Ford dealer in the county. He had quickly moved up through the ranks, eventually securing the job of managing director. He left that position in 1982 and with a young family of four kids he took the risk of going out on his own, despite the very difficult trading environment of the early 1980s. He rented a small section of a forecourt in a fuel station directly across the road from our house in Clonmel. He started in August 1982 with one car and £17,000. It was a massive decision as Ireland at the time was deep in recession, interest rates were ridiculously high and he had a very young family. But his vision was very simple. He was going to offer a one-on-one personal service and provide a range of second-hand cars that were presented to a level that left the client in no doubt of their quality, which would ensure that he could then charge more for his cars than anybody else was charging, making his sales far more profitable. And he was perfectly up front about this with his customers. He would openly admit that he was not the cheapest around, but his cars were definitely the best. And it worked brilliantly. Nobody else came close to him and he was massively successful. His decision to go solo had paid off.

By the time he offered me a job he had been up and running for four years and the business was really starting to move. My role was general runner and car cleaner, although I think he may have had a mechanical apprenticeship in mind for me ultimately. My first day was 6 January 1987. I was about to step into a brand new life.

It is such a simple statement: 'Come work with me and we'll see what happens.' It is probably said every day in this country, or some version of it, where a father or mother will casually invite a son or a daughter to work in their business. The decision to invite the kids into the family business can have a tremendously successful outcome, but more often than not, either privately or publicly, that simple decision has devastating consequences for familial relationships, marriages and even friendships. It can split the closest of families. The pain and hurt that can be caused by the crossover of family relationships with hard business decisions can be bottled up and suppressed, and may only ever surface privately, but these emotions can eat away at the people involved. From my own experience I would sound a note of caution to all parents and offspring who are thinking of making this decision. Consider this anecdote:

A very successful businessman had a meeting with his new son-in-law. 'I love my daughter and now I welcome you into the family,' said the man. 'To show you how much we care for you I am making you a 50–50 partner in my business. All you have to do every day is go to the factory and learn the operations.'

The son-in-law interrupted: 'I hate factories, I hate the noise.'

'I see,' said the father. 'Well then, you will go to the office and run some of the operations.'

'I hate office work,' said the son-in-law. 'I do not want to be stuck behind a desk all day.'

'Wait a minute,' said the father-in-law, 'I just made you

a 50–50 partner in a moneymaking organisation, but you don't like factories and you won't work in an office. What am I going to do with you?'

'Easy,' said the son-in-law. 'Buy me out!'[2]

I'm not saying it won't work out, I'm just advising caution and suggesting that you do your homework in advance. In Ireland family businesses are a massive part of the economy. Statistics show that in 2005 there were 38,927 family enterprises operating in the services sector in Ireland, employing 88,000 part-timers and 166,000 full-time staff.[3] The total turnover generated by these businesses was €49 billion. Hence family businesses cannot be ignored and in some cases can appear to be highly successful, but behind closed doors there is often another, more personal story.

My ending up employed in the family business was perhaps inevitable and this may also be the case for many others. For me I think that the seed had been planted in my subconscious as a teenager. Comments like 'You have the gift of the gab and you'll make a great car salesman' or 'You'll work with your daddy won't you?' were common when I was a young teenager. Those teachers who had given up on me would say, 'Why would you study, you'll have a job with

---

2   www.jokebuddha.com/son-in-law

3   'Overview of Family Business Relevant Issues - Ireland', Country Fiche Ireland. PDF available for download from ec.europa.eu/enterprise/policies/sme/ files/craft/family_business/doc/familybusines_country_fiche_ireland_en.pdf

Daddy for life', although I think that might have been to relieve their own guilty consciences for giving up on another kid. Anyway, I grew up thinking I could never get another job because I was too thick and assuming that I would wind up working with Dad. I don't want the same for my own children. I want them to feel that they can choose their own path, independently. So my wife and I have agreed that the family business will not be spoken about in our home. There will be no mention of car sales. We believe that it's important to encourage the kids to travel, to try to develop their own talents, and that if they really want to follow me into the family business they should discover this for themselves. Then they will have to convince us and fight for it, rather than me making the casual 'Come work with me' remark. Already my son talks about working with me, although he wants to be a professional footballer for Chelsea at the weekend and work as a salesman with me during the week! I tell him he should go for it rather than saying, 'Forget about Chelsea, come and work with me.'

The year 1986 was my first turning point. The world was changing: it was the year of Halley's Comet, talks between the USSR and the United States about an intermediate-range nuclear arms treaty started and the Mir space station was launched. For me, school was over, I had found the love of my life, I had the job that everybody had told me I'd end up with and I had given up the part-time radio job to work full-time with Dad. I was young and eager to impress, to get out into the world and prove that I was not stupid. Unwittingly, I had now determined my future trajectory – I was going to live in Clonmel, marry a local girl and follow in my father's footsteps.

Chapter 2

The Taste of
the Silver Spoon

You are only as wise as others perceive you to be.

M. Shawn Cole

There was a very definite public perception of me in our town – rich kid, full of airs and graces, working for Daddy. Thus, proving myself would be an uphill struggle – even more so as my father was successful in his own right and very well respected in the community, a pillar of society in fact. For many sons and daughters all over the world, one of the biggest challenges when following a parent into the family business is coping with constant comparison to that parent. According to businessweek.com, William Ross, a board member of the steel giant ArcelorMittal, which produces 10 per cent of the world's steel output, once said, 'A father and son in business is usually a pretty tricky, complex relationship.' Even if I had known this back in 1986, I didn't have many options. Further study wasn't an option and I hadn't been able to hold down my job as a postman or a delivery man. Unbeknownst to me, the challenges I faced when I started in Dad's business were huge: to overcome my low self-esteem, to gain respect from staff and clients, and to prove to my father that I wasn't the fucking clown that I assumed he thought I was. But I was oblivious to all this and became inexplicably angry with the job. That anger only served to make me look like a bigger fool. I said the wrong thing, did the wrong thing and always overreacted, even with customers. I soon became aware of my father's disappointment. It was becoming clear to me that despite inviting me into the business, he didn't believe that I could ever replicate his own achievements – or rather that was my perception. I believed that he thought that I didn't have the intelligence or the people skills to be successful in the business, and that the public perception was the same. I was equally reactive to what I assumed both the community and my father thought of me. In my view, overcoming a predetermined public notion of who and what you are when you are 'the boss's son' is the single biggest challenge for any offspring who assumes a role in a family business.

At this point it is worth pointing out the old adage that there are two sides to every story. I can only relate my side and I was young, immature and unable at that time to separate my view of the world from my parents' – my perception was my reality for ten years in the family business. That is not the case now.

I expect that my father did have concerns, but in the early days he wisely kept his views to himself. He never said he was disappointed in me directly, but I was sure I could see disappointment in his face and hear it in his voice. It had the makings of the classic first-generation/second-generation conflict in a family business. My dad was a very good father, and my two sisters, brother and I enjoyed a very happy childhood, but I felt that while he was straight-up and quite direct as an employer, he was the opposite as a father. By solving my problems and directing my decisions, he was effectively guiding me down a path that he had chosen. It was a form of control that I didn't recognise at first, but in the years to come it became one of the most divisive issues between us.

I strongly believe that there comes a point where you have to take a step back and let your kids decide things for themselves, make their own mistakes and learn from these. Going straight into the family business meant that I didn't get to do that and didn't have the wherewithal to recognise my father's influence and call a halt to this process. When you are young and naive you go with the flow and allow decisions to be made for you because you don't see it happening and don't know any better, but the older you get and the more experience you acquire, the more confident you become in your own decisions and choices, and the more you see the controlling influence. The more you see it, the more you hate it and rebel against it. This rebellion almost destroyed my relationship with my father because our business relationship was intertwined with our personal one. My personal rebellion became public as we worked together, and this upset my father because he hated to be perceived in a negative light by his community. He had always maintained an incredibly low profile despite his business success.

By 1988 my father had six very profitable years under his belt. His business was called Brian Mordaunt & Son Ltd (BMS) – which became Brian Mordaunt & Sons Ltd once it became clear that my brother Brian would eventually join the business, too – and it was the most successful used-car outlet in Clonmel. My father had demonstrated brilliant skill to arrive at that point. He was now opening a new purpose-built dealership on land nearby that he had purchased in 1982. It had a cutting-edge design for its time in that it had been designed and built like a house so that it could be converted in case it failed as a business. With hindsight you might say that was extremely clever, but to me it is a demonstration of two opposing business approaches. On one hand, it could be said to be a negative approach, demonstrating my father's conservative view – by having it designed this way he had created a back-up plan in case of possible failure, despite all that he had achieved over the previous six years. To me it certainly didn't demonstrate confidence in the future, even though he had just acquired the Nissan franchise, one of Ireland's biggest-selling brands. On the other hand, it could be taken to illustrate that he possessed a shrewd business instinct, took nothing for granted and was never complacent.

Six years ago I would have taken the first view. Up to that point I had always felt that my father was conservative to a fault. However, given what the country has been experiencing since 2005, I would now take the second view. I believe he was correct to approach his investment in the manner he did. His belief was always keep a reserve, pay 60 per cent, borrow 40 per cent – he was so right! I wish I had taken that view some sixteen years later. But hindsight is 20/20.

On 1 January 1988 my father, mother and myself cleaned and dusted down our new premises. It was a massive step forward, as with the new Nissan franchise we had acquired one of the top five franchises in the country, so volume was guaranteed to increase. This franchise played a pivotal role in the success of the business. Twenty-five years ago in Ireland it was all about Japanese brands. Reliability was very important to the consumer. Toyota and Nissan led the field. To cope with the anticipated increased demand because of the Nissan franchise, my dad asked me to become a salesperson. I was so excited. One shirt, tie and a pair of shiny shoes later, and the next day away I went. My brief was very simple to start with – watch, learn and keep your bloody mouth shut!

My father is the best salesperson I have ever met. I'm not convinced that I will ever come across his like again. He had been trained by Ford – even today in the car-sales business, the Ford training of the late 1960s and 1970s is renowned. In many successful motor dealerships, if you dig deep enough you will discover that the owner or founder or a key person experienced Ford training. The focus of that training was very heavily on establishing long-term relationships with customers simply by offering a one-to-one type service. This is not difficult to achieve if you are a people person, which is exactly how I would describe my father. He has a natural ability to communicate and had the patience of a saint when it came to spending time with customers and answering their questions, as well as an instinctive knowledge of how to close the pitch at just the right moment. The more I watched, the more impressed I was and the more I wanted to emulate him and make him proud. His customers loved him and he gave them all 100 per cent. He never fell out with a customer, never argued and never disagreed. He was a problem solver. He kept his opinions to himself, and with skill and expert salesmanship he ensured that if a customer had money to spend on a car again, it would be spent with Brian Mordaunt. He worked his arse off six days a week and over his career built up reserves that I can now only dream about. He did it car by car, always offering a top-quality product and service, but always ensuring that he charged appropriately for it.

These were big boots to fill. We lived and worked together so my training was 24/7. He never let up. No matter what subject we were discussing, somehow it always came back to business. By 1991 I was in awe of his skill but still lacked the experience and maturity to demonstrate it myself. I believed in everything he did and we had agreed that he would do nothing without me understanding the whys and wherefores first. By then he was in his mid-fifties and I think that he wanted to ensure that if anything happened to him that I was fully briefed. I was part of every decision, every discussion, and attended every meeting. We were inseparable and while we could talk all day long about business, it never occurred to me that we never talked about anything else. Our father–son relationship was being replaced by a solely business relationship – plenty to talk about but nothing to say. We never did anything together that wasn't work related. It didn't feel natural to be in his company unless business was involved, but then our conversation was fluent. For the first fifteen years of my life he had worked for somebody else six days a week, and for the next twenty years we were talking shop. We may well have had a very different relationship had I worked for someone else and I certainly ponder that frequently. It's the downside of mixing family with business.

I discovered a very intelligent piece of work online called 'Building Family Business Relations'.[4] It contained two particular observations that I could totally relate to. Firstly, the piece reported that 'the family culture emphasizes self-employment'. What this means is that most business owners value self-employment, so not surprisingly children are often

---

4   By Bernard L. Erven of the University of Ohio. http://aede.osu.edu/ resources/docs/pdf/45931485-9A22-4BBB-87B13245897C8635.pdf (accessed June 2011)

raised to prefer self-employment rather than working for somebody else, with the desire to be part of the ownership or management of a company dominating career decisions. The second point that stood out for me was that each family member has specific roles within the family as well as the business. Each family member also has a personal role through their hobbies, friendships, activities or social life, unrelated to anybody in the family. Family, business and personal roles often compete with each other and can cause confusion and conflict within an individual. I can relate to this in terms of my personal relationship with my father being lost to our business relationship.

While my role in the business was growing, it was becoming clear that my brother Brian, who was six years younger than me, also wanted to work in the dealership. In years to come he would go down the same path as me, with my father's encouragement. Despite the objections of my mother, who wanted him to gain experience outside of the family business, it seemed like a natural progression for Brian to join us as he absolutely loved cars. He was the one who had followed my father around the garage as a young kid. He was witty, personable, better with his hands than I was and was absolutely driven by his desire to work with cars. I did not have the same love of cars, but my options were few and far between so my involvement was born of necessity, while his was more like a vocation. As our careers progressed, Brian's love of cars remained, while I discovered mine along the way.

Brian wasn't all that interested in the business side of the dealership, whereas that fascinated me, so working together had the potential to create the perfect business relationship. I would focus on managing the business and he would focus on selling the cars. But bringing another familial relationship into the business environment created unforeseen issues and conflicts. It seemed to me that my father didn't apply the same intensity in training Brian, and managed to maintain more of a normal father–son relationship with him. This was also a real issue for my mother, but in contrast to my perception she complained to my father that Brian was not getting equal treatment. There were two sides to that argument and both parties had a point. However, from Brian's point of view he had similar issues to my own on entering the business and he also had an older brother to contend with. In the heel of the hunt, the issue faded over time because Brian was doing something that he loved. He wanted to sell cars, so our roles evolved and they suited us both – and I think it suited my father, too, because he recognised Brian's talent in the showroom.

In the early 1990s there were a number of very significant changes to European taxation, notably the introduction of vehicle registration tax (VRT), which had a hugely negative effect on the motor industry. Revenue gave a number of seminars all over the country to inform the relevant parties, so my father and I went along to debate and educate ourselves about these huge changes, along with our bookkeeper, who was also a very long-term personal friend of my father's. This was the first time I noticed a shift in our business relationship. I understood the new system easily, but my father and John struggled with parts of it, so I had to clarify or explain if they were confused. I was able to give everyday examples of the new system in practice that made sense to them. It was a eureka moment for me. It was the first time that I had ever felt, 'Yes, I get it. I understand!' It gave me great confidence.

My time learning the ropes with my father was starting to pay dividends. We were getting on very well although I'm not sure he would have agreed that the hard work and long hours of training were showing fruit just because I understood the new taxation system. He constantly pushed me and I was never sure that I was good enough – or as good as him – no matter how much I learned. I put myself under pressure to follow in his footsteps and he didn't discourage that! But I didn't yet have his experience or maturity, and I struggled with the 'boss's son' complex throughout my twenties. By now the business employed seven people, including myself and my parents, and employees who could see that this was my Achilles heel would take advantage of it and challenge me to react under pressure, and I duly obliged. This certainly didn't earn me any respect from either employees or my father. I took his criticism as negative rather than constructive – I'm not sure how it was intended to be received, but for me his criticism served to demotivate rather than motivate. I took it personally rather than as an employee receiving feedback from his boss. Boundaries are clouded in family businesses. Having said that, any negative comments remained in the back of my mind every time I entered into a new negotiation and so I tried harder with each deal in order to get a different reaction from him. His approval was very important to me and not receiving it, whether intended or not, spurred me on to get results. The silver spoon was knocked right out of my mouth. I was going to have to earn his respect.

Chapter 3

Growth Spurt

Change is the law of life and those who look only to the past or present are certain to miss the future.

John F. Kennedy

Acquiring the Nissan franchise along with our move to the new garage was really starting to pay dividends. It was the early 1990s and despite some caution around the world because of the Gulf War, there was a belief that the European economy was poised for growth and that being a member country of the European Union would deliver returns sooner rather than later. After a general election in 1994, resulting in a Labour–Fine Gael coalition led by Fine Gael's John Bruton, Ruairi Quinn was appointed minister for finance. This appointment was critical in the history of the Irish motor industry as he launched the original government scrappage scheme, offering buyers of new cars a £1,500 rebate if they scrapped a car that was ten or more years old.

This was one of the positive turning points in the industry

over the last twenty years. Volumes of new car sales in Ireland in the late 1980s averaged only 54–55,000 units annually, which per capita was one of the lowest in the world. If car sales could be stimulated, revenue streams of VAT, VRT and motor tax would flood in. This was the perfect opportunity to improve the average age profile of cars in Ireland. Up to that point there was a raft of unsafe, unsuitable old wrecks strewn across the country. The scrappage scheme was launched and it was an instant success. Sales of new cars grew year on year from that point. By 2006 Ireland was thirteenth in the world for car ownership per capita.

There was no looking back. From that point, the mid-1990s, I only ever knew growth. We were making huge profits and the more I sold and got involved in the day-to-day running of the business the more confident I became. My life was full. Anne and I were about to tie the knot and we purchased a house and moved in exactly three weeks after we were married. Plans were well advanced on the building of a new showroom at the garage – prior to that we showed cars on the forecourt and a showroom was the natural progression. It made us feel like a fully fledged motor dealership rather than a small-town garage. The business had become a major part in my life and by this time I was really enjoying it. Dad and I were proving to be a hell of a team. We were making a lot of money. I continued to watch and learn daily. We were very comfortable in each other's company. I had been involved for over seven years at that point and I felt that my input was more effective than it had ever been. I noticed that my father relied on me a little more than before, but he was still concerned that I hadn't earned the respect of our staff and inevitably we still clashed from time to time.

Our growth was undeniable so we needed to take a more proactive approach to our long-term strategy. At the suggestion of our long-time friend and bookkeeper we researched a few accountancy firms on the lookout for a whizz-kid financial expert who could look at our position and create a road map for the future and put our profits to work. We found our man and most of the advice and suggestions were very relevant. The remit was to advise on the next steps that we, as a family, needed to take given the wealth that we were starting to accumulate. The advice was to extract the wealth of the company from the company and redistribute it into our personal finances. It was time to start in the property business.

My father was advised to buy the assets of the business – the land and buildings. The bricks and mortar would be put in his name and he would rent them back to the business, thus allowing him to use the rental income to start making personal investments in property. On my twenty-sixth birthday my father completed the purchase of the property at Davis Road from the company. I was given 24 per cent of the Davis Road property, 24 per cent of the shares in the company and 24 per cent of all future property purchased by the business.

This was a turning point for me personally. It was recognition from both my parents of my accomplishments, it was an act of confidence and trust, and more importantly it was the beginning of the succession of the second generation in our family business. For many, this transition of ownership doesn't happen until after the death (or at least the retirement) of the founding member or previous generation. Yet there I was, seven years after leaving school with no qualifications, married, a home-owner, a property investor and a director and shareholder of a successful business. I was feeling very pleased with myself because I had earned it with hard work, long hours and by making a real contribution to the growth of the business despite the 'boss's son' noose around my neck. On paper I had become a very wealthy young man.

'Section 23 relief'[5] were the buzzwords of the day. The Irish economy was starting to boom and property-based tax incentives were widely available, encouraging investors to minimise their exposure to income tax. There was no better place for high-net-worth individuals to legally avoid tax on their personal income than Ireland. Within months of the transfer my parents and I had invested in our first apartment.

---

5   In general, Section 23 relief is a tax relief that applies to rented residential property in a tax-incentive area designated for 'rejuvenation'. It is available to anyone who has incurred expenditure on the purchase, construction, conversion or refurbishment of a qualifying property and who lets that property, having complied with certain conditions. Tax relief for expenditure incurred can be set against the rent received from that property and other Irish rental income so that the amount of a person's taxable income is reduced.

Little did we know it at the time, but we had just hopped onto the Section 23 merry-go-round. Buy one, rent it out and pay tax on the rent or buy another Section 23 property to offset the tax due on that rental income against the income from the first one. The problem then was that you had to buy a third to offset the rent on the second and so it went on, but we didn't get to grips with this until our property portfolio was well advanced and we were in deep. It was a frenzy. It was the beginning of the Irish property bubble, not to be confused with the Celtic Tiger, and we went on to buy houses, apartments, office space, holiday homes and shops using every available taxation scheme or incentive. I understood the pros and cons of each of the tax schemes. My father and I would debate each purchase. We would finance some and pay for others in full.

It was a great time to do business in Ireland. I could feel the change taking place across the land. Real wealth was emerging, and all the positives and negatives that go with it. As well as staying focused on growing our business, I wanted to keep abreast of the constant stream of tax-incentive packages that continued to roll out. Pensions were the new focus for tax avoidance and perhaps strangely, although I suspect it's a cultural or generational thing, many people who were at that time in their fifties and very successful had not provided for an income in their retired life. My father was one of these people, so he now began investing heavily in a pension fund. The pension legislation meant that a proprietary director could write a cheque for a considerable amount of money – for example €200,000 – from their business to their pension fund tax free. It was a tax-efficient way of taking income from a business for retirement. It was an expense to the business so it was tax deductible in company accounts – everyone's a winner. Once a large amount of money was made, there were many ways of investing it and reducing personal exposure to Revenue.

My confidence continued to grow. I had become a good salesperson and my life was progressing, but deep down I wanted more authority in the business and felt that my parents were simply too involved in day-to-day operations. They still owned 76 per cent of the business and had 100 per cent control over day-to-day operations. There were control issues, arguments and lots of conflict about daily business decisions, the repercussions of which spilled over into my personal life and had an impact on my marriage, my relationship with my siblings and parents, and my own peace of mind. There were good times and great rewards, but I don't believe that any of that is worth compromising those relationships for. Anne and I argued intensely about how I had allowed the business to become the third member of our marriage. On many occasions I would end up defending the business during our arguments or even justifying some of my father's actions or comments during rows I'd had with him. It's a complex, emotional situation to find yourself in and it can be very damaging to relationships, especially marriages. Emotionally, nothing can prepare a person for the politics and stress of working in a family business, particularly if you do so well that it becomes your career and the struggle for control becomes an issue.

The business was generating huge cash reserves, but the workload was starting to take its toll. We needed help. My father and I were doing all of the selling because my brother Brian had gone to Nissan dealerships in Wexford and Dublin for external training. We needed more staff, so we set out on a recruitment drive for sales staff to drive further growth. Nissan still commanded a very strong market share in Ireland and there was talk on the industry grapevine about a new franchise coming to the Irish market. The company that had the distribution rights for Nissan in Ireland were to acquire the rights for a new franchise called Daewoo. Daewoo had a range of cars so aggressively priced that you couldn't afford not to buy one.

After one very brief meeting with the Daewoo management team in 1998 we signed up and agreed in principle to build a new showroom – we would call it Daewoo Clonmel and it would be set up as a separate company to Brian Mordaunt & Sons Ltd. We definitely needed to extend our team. Brian was to return and work exclusively on the Daewoo brand. There was real excitement about the potential of the Daewoo franchise, which was all about offering the customer cars with significant levels of specification at prices that made a lot of sense. Once it was launched nationally it delivered on its price/spec promise.

We started interviewing. I took on the recruitment and training of our new salespeople. I hired on instinct and we set out on an aggressive training programme. I hired a sales team of three and things went well. Daewoo was an instant success. We sold 110 cars in our first year from a modest premises with no major overheads. Nissan commanded 10.4 per cent of the most buoyant car market in the history of the state. The car industry continued to boom and the millennium 00 number plates were so hot that pre-orders for the new year were going to be massive. We had our new showroom at the Nissan dealership on Davis Road, a young, dynamic sales team and our new Daewoo franchise located in a rented premises on the other side of town, being run by Brian. My father's shrewdness, banking profit since 1982, along with my youthful and dynamic approach, combined with the hefty sales volumes of the previous years, had translated into a very healthy balance sheet. Confidence on the island was at new levels. Foreign direct investment into Ireland was all the rage. Our economy was becoming the talking point of Europe, so naturally multinationals wanted to invest.

In late 1998 we had received an approach from a German supermarket chain that was not very well known at the time. They introduced themselves as Lidl. Their strategy was to open a chain of low-cost supermarkets across Ireland. They expressed an interest in purchasing 1.25 acres of land adjacent to our showroom. My father and I had never heard of Lidl, but it seemed clear to us that money was no issue for them. We had owned the land since 1982 and other than developing the house-shaped dealership had done nothing with it. After months of heavy-duty negotiation with the Germans, myself, my father and our solicitor arrived in Dublin for final negotiations with the senior management team from Germany. After hours of discussion we successfully closed the sale for a record price for land in the area by some distance – and we still had four acres of undeveloped but zoned land out of the original seven acres Dad had bought in 1982.

We closed 1999 on a high. We'd vastly increased our personal wealth with the land sale, we were National Nissan Dealer of the Year, our new Daewoo franchise was off to a flying start and so we entered the new millennium bullishly with good reason – the car market rocketed to 230,804 units sold in the year 2000, a long way from the 55,000 units of the late 1980s. Business was continuing to boom, the economy continued to grow and we were involved with every tax-incentive scheme imaginable. It was a new millennium, the year of the Sydney Olympics, Bush vs. Gore, the last competitive soccer match at the old Wembley stadium and the hundredth space shuttle mission. Closer to home, Westlife banked their seventh consecutive UK no. 1, making them the hottest pop band in Europe, the IRA started decommissioning and Bill Clinton made an historic visit to Dublin, while Shelbourne FC did the double, followed by

Kerry winning the All-Ireland in football and Kilkenny in the hurling. We were becoming very wealthy. History was made and it looked like things could only get better.

Chapter 4

Succession and Control

The optimist sees the rose and not its thorns; the pessimist stares at the thorns oblivious to the rose.

Kahlil Gibran

In the early 2000s we continued to enjoy the fruits of the economy and massive volume sales in the car industry. We marched into 2001 with both franchises performing very well. It was a volatile year in our personal relationship though, as my father and I disagreed about strategy. I had an optimistic view, my father seemed to me to be the eternal pessimist. I wanted to drive on, to invest in and grow the business, which I believed was a sound and sensible strategy given our success and the robust economy. But my father would say, 'No. No. No – for fuck sake listen to me – we have 170 used cars in stock. None of us know what's around the corner. I remember the Suez Canal crisis in 1956 – everything stopped. I remember the 1980s when interest rates were 16 per cent. You are being naive. You haven't a clue. You've only known good times.'

Over and over, year on year, it was like a broken record to me. I would think to myself, 'Jesus Christ, you are waffling on with this bullshit for four years. If we were to follow your lead, we would do nothing and go nowhere.' In reality, what was happening was that we had developed two very different agendas – he was obsessed with building a retirement fund and I wanted to take risks, expand and grow the business. Our conflicting positions were not good for the company and had a detrimental effect on family life.

Both agendas were about to be tested. It was just another day and it was time for lunch so I zoomed down the road to meet Anne for a sandwich. Dad went home. It was 1.25 p.m. on 11 September 2001. The next thirty minutes changed my world forever, and within forty days my working relationship with my father would end.

For ten years my father had been advocating a cautious approach to growing the business while I had been more inclined to take risks. 9/11 and the fallout thereafter was timely in proving that my father's conservatism would serve us well. International stock markets were suspended, oil prices rocketed and fear spread around the world like wildfire. Our business simply stopped. Deals were cancelled, refunding deposits was the name of the game now. We were blocked up with stock. We had 170 used cars, the majority of which were only months old. Everything Dad had said might or could happen, happened. It was the perfect stick to beat me with, although

I felt that 'I told you so' was unjustified because nobody could have predicted that event, nor the impact it would have on world politics and economies. I felt enormous pressure, both because of the deterioration of my relationship with my father and also because it was my first time experiencing any kind of slowdown in business – although as time would tell the post-9/11 downturn was a Mickey Mouse affair compared to the downturn of late 2008. Dad was right. Having a cash cushion in your business is the ultimate security and you do not fully appreciate that until (a) it's gone and (b) you need it.

Necessity is the mother of invention. Post 9/11 we had to refocus and get creative to survive. This necessity triggered a talent for marketing that had hitherto been dormant but that became a massive weapon in our armoury from 2001. Our marketing campaigns and adverts got us lots of publicity and resulted in debates on radio, awards, praise and criticism. Love us or hate us, the public couldn't ignore us. Competition in the industry had become fierce and we needed to separate ourselves from the rest of the pack. We had a lot of stock and for the first time we desperately needed to incentivise customers to buy from us rather than our competition.

I had the idea of creating an advert using an image that had nothing to do with a car, something so irrelevant that people would read it just to see what it was. This meant that a hell of a lot more people read the ad than would have had it been very obviously an ad for a car or a garage, which would only have been read by car buffs or people looking to buy a car. The power of advertising should never be underestimated. The most recognised global brands – Budweiser, Toyota, Coca Cola, Nokia and McDonald's spring to mind – spend millions on advertising and it works; you know exactly who they are and what they do even if you never consume their product. I learned through my adventures in advertising to be clever not bland, tenacious not timid. You should judge the success of your ad campaign based on footfall or phone traffic, because your ad will not sell your product, you will. The advert simply advises people.

Many companies run ad campaigns then complain that they didn't increase sales whatsoever as a result. I believe that this can probably be explained by a very poor ad or because the product didn't pass muster when it came to the crunch – badly priced, badly packaged or poor quality. We got creative. We didn't run our ads in the car section of the papers, we got them on the front pages, and if the ad was either daft or cryptic enough, everyone who bought the paper would read it. Our ad showed a cat caught in the headlights of a car as if about to be run over and offered customers three years' free servicing and three years' road tax with any 00 or 01-registered car purchased. It was simple, but the offer was innovative and we had the structures in place to make it work. The response was massive and we started to move our post-9/11 stock. I got a huge thrill and knew that innovative marketing would be par for the course from now on. Our competition didn't know what had hit them.

Despite this success, my father and I were still not getting on. His point had been proved, although I felt it had been the result of extraordinary circumstances, so the old conflict between caution and risk hung around. I felt like he was becoming increasingly frustrated with the perceived shift in power in the business and our conflicting agendas. It was such an emotive subject. My father had been in business in one way or another since 1961; he had achieved success as a self-employed person, had been the sole decision-maker and master of his own destiny. Now there was a silent shift of power taking place that on the one hand he wanted and needed to happen, but on the other was reluctant to accept fully. It's a powerful personal conflict and in a family-business context raises issues of legacy and trust, and can change the dynamic of the parent–child relationship. It creates inner turmoil and that can be manifested in the person's behaviour.

In the case of my father it seemed like he was angry with me all the time. I think he knew that the end of his career was on the horizon, although we didn't discuss it and neither one of us had a clue about how it would eventually happen. It was having a hugely negative effect on both our business and personal relationship and we just couldn't get through to each other. Work life was becoming unbearable and I was desperately unhappy. This spilled over into my own family life and Anne became increasingly angry with my father because of the effect that my relationship with him was having on our marriage. She believed that he was being overbearing and controlling, and that I was weak and wouldn't stand up to him – but she only ever expressed this to me and didn't discuss it with anyone else. Family relations were appalling, we were being torn apart. Something was going to have to give.

Meanwhile, business continued to improve and recover from the 9/11 fallout. My newfound passion was coming up with quirky slogans, offers and adverts. It was working like a charm and continued to stimulate forecourt activity. We had three years of selling Daewoo cars under our belt and had achieved everything we could with the brand in the rented premises. It was attracting a different client to the Nissan product. We decided to take the Daewoo brand to the next level by building a new, separate premises to house Daewoo Clonmel. It would be a wise investment in property as far as we were concerned, even though we would have preferred to keep all our brands on the one forecourt and in the one location, but back in the day this just wasn't possible. Distributors would simply not allow it. We found an ideal piece of land one mile east of our existing dealership and were to commence building in 2002.

One month after 9/11, plans for the new development were well advanced. However, there was anxiety about the global economy as a result of 9/11, and the tension between my father and myself continued to grow because of the financial commitment we were making to the new build, our stock levels and the continuous battle for day-to-day control. It all became too much and I was at breaking point – my father and I were hardly communicating. I picked up the phone to Anne and said I needed to get away for a few days and asked her to come with me. Four hours later we were sitting in a quiet hotel where we stayed for forty-eight hours and I took stock of everything. It became clear to me that one of us would have to leave Davis Road as we were no longer capable of working together, or both the business and family would suffer irreparable damage. I think he must have felt the same way because when I asked my parents to meet me to try to sort everything out they readily agreed. We all knew what the meeting would be about.

I vividly remember the time, date and conversation – the night of 17 October 2001. A heated conversation took place, then silence fell in the room. My mother looked at me and said, 'Do you want it?'

'Want what?' I asked.

'Do you want control?' she asked.

I looked at my father. He said, 'Do you?'

'Yes. I'm ready.'

As my father stared at me, with the night-time illumination of the dealership reflecting through the sitting-room windows, he said with determination, 'Do it, so. It's yours. I'll clear everything out tomorrow.'

We agreed that my father's new role would be to oversee the new showroom building and he would move in there with my brother to help get it up and running. We would meet on a monthly basis to review the management accounts for Davis Road so that he could keep an eye on progress, but the day-to-day there would be wholly under my control. I would have no role to play at the new premises for Daewoo Clonmel. I went home that night more relieved than excited, and nervous about my new responsibility. Something didn't feel right. I was sad that it had come to this.

With hindsight I think the meeting that night was all wrong. I shouldn't have placed my father in that position, giving him an ultimatum, forcing him to walk. I think he should have told me to fuck off if that's what I wanted to do! Instead, my ultimatum effectively ended his career there and then, and I didn't have the right. The alternative that night was for me to walk, but I believe that this would have upset him greatly, too. Either way there was never going to be a happy ending to that meeting. We had worked together for fifteen years. I had learned everything I knew about selling cars from him and for many of those years we had worked brilliantly together, even though we had been very hard on each other at times and our father–son relationship had been totally compromised by it.

That meeting set a new course for my father and me, and it began the next day when my father cleared out his office, taking his nameplate off his office door. Jesus Christ, I couldn't believe this was happening because of my ultimatum. I will never forget the image of my father walking out of the building onto the forecourt with just one box in his hand – carrying the remnants of his entire forty-year career. I wondered then what the implications would be for both of us.

On my first solo run the business recorded its largest profit in one year in the history of the company. I was diligent because I was so scared. I allowed nothing outside of my control. I was driven by the overwhelming need to prove to my father that I could do it. Not only that I could create profit but also that I could manage this company and be trusted. That the right decision had been made and that I was capable.

As agreed, Dad concentrated on building our new showroom. Daewoo was still performing well from the rented site. Dad never came to visit the main premises, but we would meet to talk business monthly. We didn't really see each other outside of that. I think that once he'd had time to reflect on what had happened he was disgusted with me and was asking himself how I could have done that to him. However, I felt I had little choice – one of us needed to be decisive. Looking back, we were both wrong – we were both impatient and lacked the ability to find common ground. A balance should have been achievable but seemed to be beyond us. To this day my mother says that myself and my father are very alike – both stubborn fools! While the decision that night was difficult and perhaps wrongly executed, I still wonder what would have happened to both the business and our relationship had we been able to achieve that balance.

At a family event months later somebody wanted to get a photo of the three generations of Mordaunt men together – my father, my son and myself. When Anne eventually framed that photo of the three of us, she said that there were actually four people in the image: me, George, my father and the tension. It is etched all over our faces.

Having banked massive profits in 2002, the company had significant cash reserves, a healthy used-car stock and two debt-free buildings. The business was solid and I was flying solo at Davis Road. The year 2003 brought new challenges in the motor industry because of new European law which resulted in dealerships having to qualify for new franchise contracts by meeting ridiculous criteria set by manufacturers all over Europe. Disastrous. It resulted in dealers being forced to build massive glass showrooms (that became known as glass palaces) to enhance the customer experience of shopping for a new car. Between 2004 and 2006 fancy new showrooms were popping up all over the country, but today you see many of them empty and closed, with huge debt still owing on them. The directive was known as block exemption and I believe it destroyed the best of car-sales businesses all over Ireland, and served only to make cars and servicing much more expensive for the consumer. Instead of selling cars and giving excellent customer service, we had to spend time deciding what tiles to put in the bathroom, what colour to paint the reception desk (blue with a tinge of pink here and cream there) and organising shiny signage, all of which says, 'Look at us, customer, we are mega-rich so please buy your car from us.' We had to have 1.25 sales people for every 100 cars sold and special tools for cars that we had never even sold. It was bullshit and we tolerated it because business was good and we didn't want to lose our franchises or upset the status quo.

As part of this new directive, all dealerships were served with an official termination notice and then each dealership had to reapply and qualify for its franchise all over again. This meant that franchises were effectively going to rotate. Some dealers would retire and not make the financial commitment to reapply, others would not qualify when they reapplied and yet more would not be able to raise the required working capital to build a showroom. The criteria were very specific and there was no getting around them. A dealer needed 120 square metres of showroom, full after-sale facilities with specific levels of staff based on units sold. Once I had all of the information I decided to write to the top seven distributors in the country telling them who and where we were. I felt this was a prudent move as I was taking nothing for granted with the renewal of our Nissan franchise until there was a contract sitting on my desk.

Immediately after the termination notice for Davis Road had been issued (which was the standard format for renegotiating terms to renew the franchise) I received a call from Renault, who requested a meeting urgently to explore possibilities of opening dealerships in Kilkenny or Clonmel, or both. I agreed to meet them, assuming that it would lead to a dead end but that, at the same time, it couldn't hurt. Little did I know that it would turn out to be the most expensive phone call that I ever received.

Chapter 5

Who Wants to be a Millionaire?

If your only goal is to become rich, you will never achieve it.

John D. Rockefeller

What makes a person want to be rich? The desire for riches and wealth has existed since time began. What drives this desire and what grades the desire is less clear – why are some people happy with their wealth at, say, €2 million while others do not feel wealthy until they have, say, €200 million? I suspect much of this desire lies in the need to impress, to prove to yourself and others that you have ability, intelligence and are a force to be reckoned with. Greed, the need for security or the fear of poverty could also be factors.

In 2006 I attended a summit called 'Leaders in London', where Bob Geldof was one of the speakers. He told the audience that he is driven by the fear of poverty as he remembers a period in his younger days when he and his family were poor and the fear of returning there keeps pushing him forward. Mark Zuckerberg, the founder of Facebook, has achieved such great wealth in six years that it has resulted in him becoming the youngest billionaire in the world. Why not sell up? Why risk something worth huge money peaking and eventually being sold for a far lesser amount? Why keep going? What is the driver?

For me it was definitely about proving myself. The challenge and the money were secondary to the desire to be recognised as a successful business person. That is why in 2003, even with two dealerships now open in Clonmel, I wanted to push forward.

The collapse of the Daewoo brand globally resulted in rioting on the streets of Korea, where Daewoo was a massive employer. It made headlines here in Ireland and effectively destroyed any opportunity to develop the brand, so its market share quickly ebbed away. New models from Daewoo dried up and the future of the brand looked uncertain. This was not exactly the type of publicity we needed given our recent investment. But our distributor informed us that the brand would survive and that a buyer would be found for Daewoo. Daewoo had been in Ireland for a little over three years. The only factors in our favour were that we had developed the land and built the new showroom for our Daewoo dealership without a mortgage, and, with only my father and brother working there, so far it had very small overheads. The only option was to put the head down, work away as best we could and hold on.

Meanwhile, Nissan was performing well with new model launches, and the car-sales market was still robust. The Irish economy was very strong and I felt vigorous, powerful and confident. I was thirty-four and had discovered an entrepreneurial streak that was addictive. I had inherited and developed a business model I believed in and I wanted to continue to expand and grow – I could see no reason not to and my father wasn't around to hold me back now. I wanted to get deeper market penetration in Clonmel and also take our business further afield. Then the call came from Renault. Feeling bullish, I met with them even though I didn't really expect much to come out of the meeting. I loved their product, and, despite a few reliability problems with the line over the years, the model range had grown and Renault's market share was on target to hit over 7 per cent of a very strong car-sales market sooner rather than later.

I immediately hit it off with their representatives. They liked my style and I liked the plans they had set out for the next five years. I decided to seriously consider their offer. They wanted a one-acre site developed in Clonmel, a premises built housing only Renault product, according to an agreed Renault design, and staff recruited and trained. In return I would receive a contract right up to 2008, which would be renewed if all Renault criteria and standards were maintained.

The benefit for me was that this deal would see the business acquire another 7 per cent of the Tipperary market as this would be the only Renault franchise in all of south Tipperary and would make us the biggest motor dealer in the county. However, there were problems to be considered too:

(a) It would be the third Mordaunt motor dealership in Clonmel: was that sensible or would it be overkill?

(b) I would need to spend over €2 million to get the entire project up and running – this would have to be financed and I had learned a hard lesson about cash reserves after 9/11.

(c) How would a deal with Renault affect our existing relationships with Nissan and Daewoo, and would it dilute our performance in either franchise?

(d) Could I handle the expansion personally?

On the flip side, I believed that if I didn't do this somebody else would assume the role and with it the additional 7 per cent market share. Car sales continued to grow, I was young, confident and had a dream of turning our company into a motor group in different locations by the time I was forty. So it was difficult to turn down the Renault deal despite my concerns. I began to see it as a win-win situation, and using a previously tried-and-tested method of investing in the national obsession that was property at that time, the deal would also allow me to build the building and rent it to the business. My logic was that I would end up with a profitable new dealership with a strong brand as well as another sound investment in property. It was a winner.

I would have liked to seek advice from my father, but by then our relationship had further deteriorated as we had had another row, this time over the purchase of a site for a new home that Anne and I wanted to build. It was a truly magical site, hidden from the road and accessible through a wooded grove. I loved it. The property boom was just starting and it became clear that this site would sell for huge money. It was 2.2 acres and was going to auction with a reserve of €144,000. I bought the site at auction for what became a record in Clonmel for residential land. My father thought I was mad. He was angry, but I'm not entirely sure why as I bought the land with my own funds. Maybe it was because of the price I had paid and the profile and publicity it had created – he was such a private person. Nine months later half an acre was selling for exactly the same money. We designed and built a beautiful home and moved into it in 2004. It remains one of our best ever decisions, but it drove a further wedge between my father and me.

I had fifteen months to find a one-acre site, build a 9,000-square-foot premises, recruit ten staff and be open for business by late 2004. I needed to borrow serious money for the first time. I wrote a business plan on two pages of a child's copybook and that combined with a two-hour meeting with senior bank officials secured a sanction of over €2 million, with the premises itself as security. I purchased a magnificent site within eight weeks, hired a top-quality architect and we were on our way.

Renault loved our efficiency. There had been good re-presentation of the Renault product in Clonmel as a dealer had been operational there for years, but Renault decided not to renew that franchise. Public opinion was that I had somehow swiped the franchise from the other local dealer, but that wasn't the case. Renault came to me. I was offered the opportunity. Small-town Ireland being what it is, I ignored the rumour mill and the begrudgers and got on with the business, employing local people and providing an excellent facility, product and service. As 2004 rolled around I worked closely with my team at our main dealership, preparing them for the fact that my time was going to have to be split across dealerships now. Committed and driven key staff, who are trustworthy and reliable, are vital to any expansion in my experience.

I was now so focused on business that it had the potential to consume me. I had become a workaholic. I loved Monday mornings when everybody else hated them. I had a whole week ahead to duck and dive, pit my skills against others, look at opportunities and make money. I loved the challenge. I was driven – in fact, I was over-driven, and I wanted more and more. Those were great times to be in business in Ireland. I felt I could not make a bad decision. However, while confidence is an important attribute in business, it can be very dangerous if it mutates into ego that is not controlled – ego has its place but it must be managed and there is a very fine line between confidence and ego.

By now my ego was taking over. I had become caught up in the ridiculous consumerism of the Celtic Tiger and believed I was a captain of industry and that the good times would continue to roll. At one point I wanted to buy an investment residential property, which was par for the course at the time. So I went to a local building site where eight semi-detached houses were being built. They looked nice and I felt that the development had potential as an investment. Any rational person would buy one and kit it out, taking a long-term view on the return on investment in terms of rental income, but I wanted the entire estate. I was quite convinced that I could control the entire project – set the value of the houses, control the rental income and calibre of client, as well as negotiating a larger discount from the builder with this bulk buy. I would have needed to borrow 110 per cent of the total value of the development and know I would have been sanctioned, based on previous applications. Thankfully, when I tried to buy the eight houses, four had already been sold. But I still went ahead and purchased the other four. It was insanity, but I was not alone in this craziness. I had based the decision on three things, which were rampant in Ireland at the time:

1. Access to credit finance for more than the value of the property – no regulation.

2. My ego and confidence in the economy fuelled by blatant consumerism, greed and the property bubble.

3. Living in a business bubble where, with the exception of the blip after 9/11, I had only experienced growth and was oblivious to the possibility of a reversal of fortune.

Imagine going home to your wife and telling her you had bought four houses that day? It beggars belief but it felt perfectly rational at the time. I have to face up to the reality of that responsibility now, of course, and deal with it. The government of the day led us to believe that this country had huge surpluses of cash[6] and a banking system that was closely monitored by the regulator. If so, then lending 110 per cent for the purchase of four residential properties shows systematic failure of government regulation. Who is being held accountable and responsible for that? I am taking responsibility for my actions by dealing with the debt, but who is taking responsibility for theirs? I am very angry and resentful that while the consequences of my overconfidence and greed will have a ruinous effect on my personal finances for the rest of my life, my partners in crime, so to speak, equally guilty, greedy and overconfident, are bailed out by me and my children. Why am I the only one paying the

---

6   www.tradingeconomics.com/ireland/cash-surplus-deficit-current-lcu-wb-data.html

price for a joint responsibility? The banks are institutions but there are people behind them who made those decisions. Those people are not sharing the responsibility for their role in this. Only their customers, their one-time golden boys, have a noose around their necks, while those bankers and politicians shuffle off with their massive pensions but no integrity and not a shred of dignity. At least the rest of us still have that.

Over a seven-year period, I bought eleven houses and sold four, followed by purchases of a retail shop unit, a brand-new crèche, and a share in property consortiums in Germany and Washington. I was also building my own new house and creating a new concept in barber shops called 'Get Your Locks Off', while successfully negotiating the acquisition of the Kia and Renault franchises and, as a result of this, building four new motor dealerships and assembling a fifty-strong team of management and staff – all of this before actually going to work and selling a car. I was working my arse off and despite all of this always looking to do more. My workload had trebled and I needed help, so I assembled what I saw as a task force with key, loyal staff, and I set up a new company called GBM (G – George, B – Brian, M – Mordaunt). My father was not to be involved in our Renault venture and had insisted that it be set up as a separate company. So now the family business consisted of three companies: BMS, Daewoo Clonmel and GBM.

GBM was to have a core staff of nine and I had to work out

what I would use as working capital. Over the previous ten years we had sold car finance to many customers when they bought from us. We had acted as an agent for many different banks, arranging finance for our customers with the various banks and receiving a commission from them. We had a very strong sales record in this area. The vast majority of our sales were on behalf of one particular financial institution so I approached them with a three-year plan, proposing that we would sell €10 million of retail finance in that time period.[7] I offered them 80 per cent of that business. I approached two other banks, offering them the other 20 per cent. In return I was looking for an advance of €2 million. Between two banks I received cheques totalling €2 million combined. GBM was almost ready to go and the new Renault building looked fantastic.

With the team in place and finance arranged, GBM opened in November 2004 and we invited the schools in Clonmel to take part in a colouring competition to help launch the dealership. I called to selected classes in every school in Clonmel and presented the kids with a specially designed sheet of drawing paper that had nothing on it but four wheels. They had to design the car of their dreams and present their drawing in person at the dealership, where it

---

7   Our dealership was a sales agent for many finance houses/banks and we were incentivised to sell finance to the customer once they decided to buy a car. If a car was sold for €9000 and the finance was arranged by us on behalf of the client, we would refer to that loan as retail finance.

was put on display for two weeks. At the end of the two weeks a local artist was asked to review the drawings to select the best three, allowing the kids and their schools to win prizes. The parents of the overall winner would win the use of a new Renault for one year. It was an incredibly simple but massively successful marketing campaign. Kids arrived home from school with sheets of GBM-branded paper, telling their parents they could win a free car if the child won the drawing competition, so the parents were compelled to find the new dealership so that their child's drawing could be presented. The name GBM was all the talk, especially among parents across the five schools. The grand final of the competition was to happen on a Sunday and drew a huge crowd. Crowd control was the order of the day on the opening weekend and it was a phenomenal success. It was a slick, professional launch culminating in a gala opening evening to which we invited 200 guests. I had discovered the power of marketing and invested in it. We had our own marketing department in-house. Our marketing and advertising became a massive talking point in the area. When Renault's marketing department came to view our set-up and organise the post-launch marketing and we showed them our plans, they were blown away.

Very quickly, GBM became recognised as a quality motor dealership in Clonmel. In the three years since my father had left Davis Road, the Mordaunt brand was setting the trend, we were the organisation to watch, with a young, energetic team, great marketing, great customer service and great locations; we dominated the local market. Between all three franchises – Nissan, Chevrolet (Daewoo had been rebranded at that point and Daewoo Clonmel had been rebranded as Mordaunt Chevrolet) and Renault – we had captured almost 20 per cent of the market, even with Chevrolet still struggling given its global collapse. The launch of GBM felt like a personal victory. My net income had doubled within the previous two years and my statement of affairs was looking strong. I was thirty-seven years old and felt optimistic about the future.

Meanwhile, Anne was getting itchy feet. Having stopped working in 1997 when Emily was born, she felt that the time was right to follow her dream to open a boutique. She had always had great fashion sense and there was a gap in the market in Clonmel for a good-quality boutique. Neither one of us knew anything about that business but we were sure we could learn – my confidence was at an all-time high and I was sure I could learn the ropes in any new venture.

While Anne was setting out on her project, I secretly aspired to open a fourth dealership, this time in Kilkenny. As had happened in Clonmel, there was a change of dealer in Kilkenny, and Renault were looking for a dealer to replicate our success. There was strong competition from other dealers in Clonmel, but the market appeared to me to be fairly untapped in Kilkenny. A business park was being developed in a good location, within which there was to be a 'motor boulevard', meaning that there would be sites available in the business park with planning available for four or five motor dealerships. There was a lot of interest in the sites, but nobody had actually purchased yet. I was still very ambitious to expand and I believed that a dealership in Kilkenny would grow our overall market share. My growth plans were definitely very long term, but I liked the challenge that the Kilkenny opportunity presented.

The dilemma was that under the aforementioned EC directive I would need to upgrade our Nissan facilities in Clonmel. We would need a bigger workshop and parts area and would have to deal with a flooding problem because we were closing for days at a time because of flooding. The only option for improving the Davis Road property and dealing with the flooding problem was to knock everything down and rebuild. GBM had just opened in Clonmel. Twenty-four months earlier we had opened the Chevrolet showroom and we had built it with no mortgage. I wanted a Renault dealership in Kilkenny and would also have to invest massively in Davis Road. But everything was doing well, everything was performing. The economy showed no sign of slowing down. It was decision time. I decided to go for it.

I secured the finance with ease but had to use Mordaunt Chevrolet as security. With the money raised I purchased the land in Kilkenny and started a new build at Davis Road. When I first hired the builder to build our original Daewoo premises it was February 2002 and we had two buildings debt free. By the time all four dealerships, along with my new house, were complete it would be January 2007 and three of the four dealerships had an attached debt.

At this point we were again carrying a huge level of used stock. The car-selling industry was very much dictated by the manufacturer or distributor. Very lucrative incentives were placed before dealers and we were expected to participate. Incentives were paid on registrations rather than sales, so when newspapers reported that car sales were up, say, 18 per cent, it was registrations of cars that were up, not necessarily sales, and this is why on any forecourt between 2004 and 2009 you would have seen plated cars with no mileage on them for sale. In turn, dealers offered great deals to the consumer in order to shift the new car and reduce the dealer's exposure by replacing it with a used car, albeit it an expensive used car. Carrying over a large stock of used cars is an issue in itself, but not managing the rotation of this fleet is extremely dangerous because cars depreciate in value so quickly. For example, a salesperson will trade in a 07-registered Nissan Primera if it will get them a sale, despite the fact that the dealership might be carrying six or seven of the same car from that same year in stock. I was worried about the level of stock that was on site at the Nissan dealership in 2005. It needed more control and attention than I was giving it as I was very distracted with the new development in Clonmel, with the potential development in Kilkenny and with the new Renault franchise that GBM was now operating.

GBM had a full team of staff, as had BMS. By December 2005 the upgraded Nissan dealership was ready to open and we had a spectacular launch of our newly revamped headquarters on Davis Road. Two hundred guests were invited. A jazzy cabaret was the theme. The building looked amazing. It was a real local landmark. In the few short years since my father had left, we had grown at a rapid pace. Despite relations not being any worse between us, they were not much better either, but he liked the new dealership. He told me that he felt that we had created something to be proud of. I was happy with how everything was going and delighted with our new HQ.

There was only one thing making me feel slightly uneasy on that opening day. I had looked at our bank balance earlier in the day and was surprised to see that we had practically no cash. It seemed that our once very healthy funds had disappeared overnight. I realised that this was the downside to having three companies trading. There's nothing like the car business to soak up cash. A typical scenario to explain this is, say, each of our seven salespeople across the three businesses sells a new car and each sale generates a trade-in. Assuming all those new cars are delivered on the same day, they all have to be paid for by the dealer on the same day, but at the same time there can be quite a time lag between the dealer paying the manufacturer for the new car and the customer paying the dealer. However, I dismissed my uneasy feeling, telling myself that it was just a temporary cash-flow glitch for this reason. After all, any talk of a slowdown was years away and even if it did actually arrive I believed that it would be nothing more than that – a slowdown.

My relationship with both our distributors and our financial partners was very strong. I never bullshitted them. I was always very open and transparent in my dealing with them when looking for finance, and in meetings they referred to this and said they appreciated it. I was an important customer and was frequently invited to presentations about various schemes that they organised. In 2007 a bank invited me to a presentation that was to take place in Waterford Castle. At that gathering I was introduced to a concept I had not heard of before: the CFD (contract for difference). This was a unique way of buying shares. Essentially, if you could prove to the bank that your net personal value was greater than €2 million, you received an open-ended sanction that allowed you to buy a large volume of shares, but using a CFD you only had to pay out about 15 per cent of the value of the shares yourself. The other 85 per cent was borrowed. The objective was to gamble on the movement of the share price of the large amount of shares that you purchased.

I loved the concept and couldn't wait to get started. I traded blue-chip shares, especially AIB and Anglo-Irish Bank, safe bets, and would buy anything up to 24,000 shares at a time. If the share price during the day increased by 20 per cent I would cash in and bank the profit. If the share price fell by 20 per cent I would inject more funding to maintain the correct levels of equity.[8] At the start I was borrowing up to 90 per cent and only paying 10 per cent for any shares that I bought. I bought my first shares at €24 each. I lost €3,000 on the first day. Within ten days I had bought more shares, sold them two days later and banked a profit of about €3,000 so I had broken even early on.

Once I felt I understood the concept and the market I started to concentrate heavily on the movement of share prices at Ryanair and AIB. It became addictive. I ensured I was at my desk with my computer on for the opening of the markets every day and watched the fluctuations all day. I loved the buzz of the buying and selling. Within weeks of starting I was €25,000 in profit. At one stage we were taking a family holiday to Spain and before I boarded the flight I bought AIB shares and instructed my broker to sell them if they reached a certain price. They did so and he sold. By the time I landed in Spain I was €10,000 better off. It was easy money. I'd lose money some days and make money other days, but I'd generally end up quids in. Brokers told me that

---

8   For example, if I bought 25,000 AIB shares at €18 I would require funding of €450,000. I would need to advance 10 per cent in cash so I would transfer €45,000 as a deposit. The bank had effectively allowed me to borrow the balance of €405,000. I took a short-term view, so if the share price went up by, say, 20 cent I would sell all my shares and make a profit of €5,000, less a small fee and some tax. This could happen over any time period, from one hour or two days or a week, and I might have even purchased and/or sold twice in the same day. The rewards were huge but the losses could be equally large. Using the same example but with a reduction in the share price of 20 cent, I would be required to transfer €5,000 to the bank instantly in order to maintain a minimum 10 per cent deposit on the value of the borrowing.

it was as safe as houses because I was dealing in blue-chip shares. Little did I know!

Meanwhile, Anne was busy getting her boutique ready to trade. She had been successful in signing up some exclusive brands that were not previously available in Clonmel and she opened her business in September 2005. It hit the ground running. She had done it all herself, having known nothing about the fashion business when she set out and knocking on doors all over the UK and Ireland learning the ropes step by step. A real entrepreneur. I was delighted for her. By the time Christmas came we were both exhausted. What a year it had been. Life was very different for both of us now. Hard work and long hours were the name of the game, but we were determined not to lose focus on our family life. We had agreed from the beginning that despite the long working hours that being self-employed would require, family life was very important and we did not ignore the responsibilities of having two young kids.

There was so much to be positive about. By now we were in our second year in our new home, GBM had been very well received, our new Nissan showroom looked fabulous and removing the risk of flooding was a huge relief. Daewoo was rebranded as Chevrolet by their new owners, General Motors, so there was reason to be hopeful that the return on investment there would improve. Anne had just finished her first five months trading, which had included a lucrative Christmas period, and we were also the proud owners of 1.25

acres of land which had just been approved for planning for the development of a 10,000-square-foot motor dealership in Kilkenny. There would be a lot to do in 2006.

Chapter 6

Cash-strapped

Money will buy you a pretty good dog, but it won't buy the wag of his tail.

Henry Wheeler Shaw

During the boom years I found it very difficult to find staff. They were simply not available and you had to headhunt – that's bloody expensive. I needed salespeople who were mature, ambitious, talented, prepared to put the hours in and who wouldn't tell me after a year of training them that they were heading off travelling for a year – this had been endemic with staff in the Celtic Tiger era. Over a four-year period I hired almost twenty salespeople. Of the twenty, only three came with experience; all the others had to be trained, which is a significant investment for an employer. However, I'd rather invest in training 100 honest employees than take a chance on one who was in any way hooky. My management style was to let the team get on with their job and to reward performance based on results – it was a style based on trust.

I didn't believe in micro-management, but there needs to be a balance and my laissez-faire approach cost the business dearly. Cash was tight enough after the launch of our new HQ and our systems for stock control and cash management were clearly not good enough. On one morning alone we found ourselves down €40,000 cash, and this turned out to be just the tip of the iceberg. When customers began calling looking for the extras that had been promised, anxiety hit me – how much more would this end up costing? I was furious with myself for having missed this, allowing it to happen. I had learned another hard lesson and the business had taken a massive hit in its bank balance to the tune of €160,000, which even a business with deep cash reserves would find difficult to absorb.

Anne and I often joke about what we did with our time when we were first married – we had four years of living together before we had Emily and I honestly can't remember how we filled our time! Young kids take up all of your time and a night on the town costs you the next morning when you have young kids, so when we look back at all the free time we had then we regret not enjoying it more, but of course you don't realise that at the time. The same thought occurred to me recently when thinking about my bank balance. I found myself sitting at home on a Friday evening with a glass of wine, trying to remember all the nights I came home from work over the last few years when I had plenty of cash in the business. Since cash has become my number one priority I realise that the lack of it causes incredible feelings of commercial insecurity, so I wonder when I came home every night in those good years did I experience the opposite feeling, did I feel utterly secure and did the comfort that gave me make me wasteful? Over the last three years I have often reflected on how I spent all that money, the waste, the Celtic Tiger cheque, the sheer stupidity.

There was sensible spending, too – investment in staff and training – but there was plenty of unnecessary, lavish spending, like bringing four salespeople to Las Vegas for five days to attend the North American Dealer Association conference, which was attended by motor dealers from across the United States to hear keynote speakers, attend seminars, etc. I wanted to go to learn, and rightly so, but I should have gone alone. The trip cost me €12,000.

Nothing is spent on any form of luxury in a start-up business today. When I was building I stopped at nothing short of the best furniture for our offices, computers, TVs and coffee docks for customers and, of course, art for the showrooms. Yes, art. Fancy cars for the sales team – sports cars and SUVs were the norm for them and for me; if I wasn't driving a new Mercedes Benz, it was a brand-new top-of-the-range BMW. I bought a BMW for €120,000 and sold it eighteen months later for €45,000 only to turn around and treat myself to a top-of-the-range Mercedes Benz costing €185,000 immediately afterwards. I justified it all to myself, telling myself that I could afford it and that I had worked hard to build up a company that could afford to look after both myself and my staff. The philosophy of a foolish man.

I don't accept the idea that 'times were different then' or 'that was the good old days'. That's bullshit – it was wrong, it was foolish and greedy and utterly wasteful. I and people like me borrowed, built, invested, gambled and subsequently lost. Along the way our risk-taking created huge employment and generated massive revenue for the Exchequer. I believe that we made a contribution to improving many aspects of this country, but I also fully acknowledge that we simply blew too much cash. The country was utterly consumed in its own bullshit. It didn't cost me two thoughts to blow €5,000 on the Christmas party. My company was no different to the next one at that time – I was too casual in how I handled money and I'm paying the price for that today.

I had become obsessed with amassing wealth, but for some reason that is still beyond my comprehension I didn't notice that the opposite was in fact happening. It is very clear to me now that I had no appreciation of cash in the good days nor did I realise the peace of mind it can give a business owner personally. Fear among the self-employed stems from the dilution of cash reserves. A business owner could handle any downturn, adjust and rationalise their company on many different fronts to survive, but only when it has a cushion of cash. I respect the companies that sat on their cash in the good times. There are many who very wisely continued to control overheads, make profit and bank cash piles. They are the companies that have or will move forward and get through the recession.

Ireland – its people, banks and industry – are now starved of cash and understand how important it is now more than ever. The self-employed definitely understand the stability and peace of mind that it brings. I sense that, as a people, we now fully appreciate just how reckless we were, and while we believe that the country's downfall wasn't the responsibility of the Irish consumer, Irish people accept that in a small way each and every one of us played a part in contributing to the culture of excess that came with the Celtic Tiger. I like to call it the era of Celtic greed, as evidenced by the fact that the government had to incentivise the population to save money! The Special Savings Incentive Account (SSIA) scheme is the last time I recall any government being proactive and initiating something positive for the people. If I am lucky enough to continue in business over the next twenty years, my top priority will be not to forget what it was like to have no cash in the business and no disposable income. When my father would say 'Cash is King' I would roll my eyes and ignore him. I should have listened. He had travelled this road before. No doubt we will travel it again.

By the late summer of 2006 the business was recovering from the impact of our loose systems on cash flow. By then

I was completely focused on the development of the new dealership in Kilkenny. It was time to renew negotiations with the banks on refinancing our working-capital requirements. The business in Kilkenny would gain us market share in the Carlow, Portlaoise and Wexford markets, so we targeted those towns with marketing and advertising. The retail finance deal we had done in 2004 had raised funds of €2 million for the company. This time around I wanted to do a similar deal on a three-year advance arrangement but based on four dealerships this time – our Nissan HQ in Clonmel, Chevrolet in Clonmel, Renault in Clonmel and Renault in Kilkenny.

But there was a problem. Renault wanted us to work with their finance partner when selling retail finance at the franchise in Kilkenny, but I hadn't intended to approach them with the proposal as they hadn't been interested in the deal back in 2004 when we set it up in Clonmel, and we had gone with two other financial institutions. But we wanted to keep Renault onside as I anticipated a long and mutually beneficial relationship with the franchise, so I asked the bank to quote for the business. We worked out a finance deal on the condition that security other than a personal guarantee would be given. While I would have preferred not to have given any additional security, I felt I had no choice if I wanted to proceed with the new dealership in Kilkenny. The additional security agreed was a chattel mortgage over the used-vehicle stock held at both GBM and the new Renault dealership in Kilkenny.[9] I reluctantly agreed to both that and a personal guarantee because I believed that we could repeat the success we had had in Clonmel selling retail finance over the course of the next three years.

Two banks were very anxious to do business with us – the first partner who had worked with us on the same deal in Clonmel in 2004 and now a second, who came on board when we opened the Kilkenny dealership. Between them they advanced funds of just under €2 million for the new development as well as providing working capital for GBM and BMS. The entire amount of the loan was advanced interest-free on the condition that each of the four dealerships met their agreed targets for selling retail finance for each bank. We launched our own website specifically designed for used cars only and rebranded ourselves as the Mordaunt Group, hosting three franchises in four locations. We scheduled the opening of our new venture in Kilkenny, which would be called GBM Cityside, for December 2006, just in time for the 2007 new-car market. However, for the first time in the history of our trading, business had slowed down somewhat over the previous six months. We had huge levels of stock. Despite our expectations, Chevrolet had never really recovered from the Daewoo collapse. Nissan had slipped in market share. Renault's market share had collapsed

---

9   A chattel mortgage is a security-backed loan specific to the asset and linked by the use of a serial/chassis/VIN number.

due to an aging model profile and the commencement of the transition from Irish ownership to French ownership, about which rumours were rife in the industry. This trend was emerging in the Irish motor industry in other brands as well, whereby distributors were being replaced with direct distribution from the manufacturers. How would all of this effect 2007? Time would tell, but after a year of building a new team and development of two new premises, it was time for a well-earned break over Christmas. I'd worry about 2007 when it came.

Chapter 7

Losing Control

Drive thy business or it will drive thee.

Benjamin Franklin

As 2007 began we had great hopes for the year ahead. We had an exceptionally strong brand, and our rapid expansion combined with our strong marketing had resulted in a strong regional profile. We continued to innovate and offer our customers deals and plans that could trigger substantial phone and forecourt traffic. Our stock levels were still pretty high but I never worried about how that level of stock might affect our cash flow because all we had to do to stimulate sales was come up with a great consumer offer and get it into the press.

Some of our concepts were fantastic. They were brilliantly created and the design was so good that at one point when we were consistently advertising on the back page of a local tabloid people would buy the paper just to see what this week's back-page offer was. We offered things like half-price cars, three years' free servicing and three years' road tax, double cash-back, buy a six-month-old car and get another one free. One memorable initiative was a mailout of 1,000 keys to 1,000 existing customers, with a letter telling them that this was the key to their next car – we had a car in the showroom and if their key opened it the car was theirs absolutely free.

These ideas and more all came from our own staff. I had put together a team of creative young people and if you left them all in a room to come up with ideas together, you could be sure that the very best of ideas would flow. Once we captured the idea, myself and our designers would pull it together visually. When that was complete we would decide how best to actually sell it face to face. Brainstorming the concept was vital and the production of the point-of-sale material was also critical, but at the end of the day if the salespeople couldn't nail it when the customer was sitting across from them, then it failed.

We were getting our message out there. Our aim was to get to the point where if anybody wanted to buy a car in the south-east of Ireland the first name they would think of was Mordaunt. I believe we had achieved this. We constantly carried out market research to help us stand out from the crowd and set ourselves apart from our competition. We travelled to many locations around the world looking at different concepts. Our spending with local media was huge.

Over a three-year period we had a number of firsts,

including the first-ever dedicated used-car website. This site did not include all the waffle often associated with car-selling websites, such as booking a test-drive or booking a service. It was commissioned solely to profile the used cars that we held in stock across the four dealerships, which by the end of 2007 had a combined value of €4 million. Ours was the first website to allow the customer to buy a car online. Other firsts included lifetime free road tax and service, a dealership open seven days a week in Clonmel, an in-house graphic-design studio and an in-house market-research department. We were the first local dealer to have a 'sale' of new cars rather than just of used cars. You couldn't ignore the Mordaunt brand in that region. I was proud to have created not just a group of motor dealerships but a dynamic motor organisation with everything we needed in place to keep us at the cutting edge.

On the outside it was perfect, well funded, very well presented and led by a very high-paid management team. The one thing that was missing was profit and I was beginning to worry about this consistent trend. I've heard the proverb 'turnover is vanity and profit is sanity' a million times in the last two years, and it's so true. I suspect that many business owners would find it difficult to pinpoint the moment that they started to lose control because it can be the result of a number of small things that take time to appear, and even if they manage to pinpoint one issue you might find if you dig a little deeper that it was probably only the straw that broke the camel's back. If I had been asked in mid-2007 if I was losing control of my company, I would have said absolutely not. But turnover can be very deceptive and can camouflage liquidity issues if cash isn't managed very carefully. Cash is king, as noted by Pehr G. Gyllenhammar, Volvo's CEO when referring to the global stock-market crash of 1987.

When I try to pinpoint the moment when I lost control, I would say it was from the point when I stopped buying and selling cars myself, when I delegated the responsibility for actual trading. That essentially decided our profitability. The average age of the team then was about twenty-eight. I had effectively allowed some very young people to dictate what margin we retained out of annual sales exceeding €33 million. Taking my eye off the ball in that area certainly eroded our cash, too, but the real consequences of my neglect didn't surface until our turnover started to slow down significantly – worryingly, in fact. When turnover slows down as dramatically as it did for many businesses in Ireland from 2008 to 2011, it can have a detrimental effect on cash flow. Once cash flow becomes strained, you start to do things like selling stock for the sake of making a cash lodgement rather than for profit, and once you enter that phase, it will likely be only a matter of months before it's all over for your business. So losing control for me came down to the following factors, which I had delegated to others, and that's really maddening, but I must take responsibility for it as the employer:

1. Neglecting to oversee the buying and selling of cars and ensuring that a satisfactory margin was retained.
2. Actively managing stock levels and stock mix.
3. Maximising every sales opportunity while maintaining our excellent standards in customer service.
4. Presenting our stock as though it were on display in a shop window on the high street.

In the three years from 2005 to 2008 our stock levels and stock mix were unrealistic. We ended up with over 250 used cars, a great number of which were duplicates, such as having twenty 2007-registered Renault Meganes and fifteen 2008-registered Nissan Micras. A lot of the stock was aged, meaning that it had been devalued, and the presentation of much of it was well below our established standards. I did not have a stock 'write-down' policy. Instead, we introduced consumer offers, which was my preference for liquidating stock. Every time we went to press with a consumer offer, we genuinely offered a decent price reduction or added value with a free package like servicing or road tax – often we combined both. But this soon led to a situation where we couldn't sell unless there was a freebie to incentivise a purchase.

The days of not needing skills and talent in sales – because there were plenty of customers who would buy so long as the price was in any way acceptable – were over and the gaps in our skillset appeared. If a trade-in was not managed correctly or if the cost of change, meaning the price the customer pays to upgrade their car, was wrong, that deal would probably generate a loss – in some cases we would accept this because there were back-end deals for dealerships from the distributors which would offset the loss.[10] The industry was driven by distributors. The aim was to sell big numbers to receive a fat bonus in the form of a registration rebate, so when we got close to achieving the target they had set for us, but were shy of the requisite number of cars sold, we would register a load of cars to get over the line. We'd get the bonus but wind up with, say, twenty new cars registered but not sold. So we'd advertise them with thousands of euro off to try to offload them. Those deals, known as pre-reg deals, resulted not only in losses, but were usually accompanied by a badly priced trade-in because of pushing the sale through to offload the pre-reg, and away we went, heading for even deeper losses. The organisation had too many cars. I knew it but could do very little without making big losses on sales of used cars.

The year 2007 had its positives. Our new venture in Kilkenny had started well. Our operations in Clonmel were performing in that we were selling, or 'shifting metal' as is said in the

---

10 The motor industry is driven by volume, with the market share of any brand being a key target. To help achieve targets, dealerships would be offered an incentive whereby if the dealership achieved a certain level of new-car registrations of a particular brand, the distributor would pay a bonus commonly known as a rebate/volume registration bonus.

trade, and we were all earning a week's wage, but we weren't making money anymore. That had stopped once I took my eye off the ball and focused on the new buildings. BMS had stopped making any real profit once I started the Renault expansion. The rapid growth we had experienced from 2003 to the end of 2007 hadn't resulted in massive profits, but we had access to unconditional borrowings because of the strength of our business up to that point and the presumption that a brisk trade would continue. It was a false economy, which is an accurate reflection of what was happening in the national economy, too.

With our borrowings we expanded and grew the business while simultaneously developing a small property portfolio. My lifestyle improved immeasurably, but my business didn't actually benefit in any real way during the boom because I was so caught up with expansion. That is a huge regret. It was a wasted opportunity to make real profits and build a cash reserve, as had been repeatedly advocated by my father. When the economy collapsed, a cash reserve would have served me well, rather than valueless property and those borrowings stifling the business. My lifestyle, like so many others, had to change and the one place that for years I had been able to turn to for help if I needed it, the family business, had not seen the tangible benefit of those good years, so there was nothing left to help me with.

Despite the rebrand of Daewoo to Chevrolet, there was only limited hope of a recovery of sales of the brand. In spite of our best efforts, throwing time and money at our smallest showroom for five years, as insisted upon by the then Daewoo distributor, nothing had worked. We needed to change something at that dealership. We needed to find a second franchise to sit alongside Chevrolet to get footfall through the doors.

Another extremely worrying threat on the horizon was media speculation that the Green Party, newly in government, had plans to make their impact on Irish life with the introduction of a new system of taxation on new cars from 2008, whereby the amount of VRT that would be payable on a vehicle would be based on the CO_2 emissions it would generate. The smaller and more efficient the engine, the lower the VRT and road tax would be and, conversely, the bigger the engine size, the higher the VRT and road tax due. The concept was sensible, but the implementation, when it came, was disastrous. In fact, I believe that the difficulties that motor dealerships have experienced, and which continue to cause havoc for so many family-owned dealerships in the industry, can be traced back not to the global financial meltdown, but are a result of the mismanaged, short-sighted approach to this project taken by the Green Party.

In summary, the new system meant that every car, under the new regulation, had a price adjustment, so if a dealership had twenty of the same used-car model, the value of that stock could be affected, either positively or negatively, depending on its emissions. The same applied to every privately owned car parked in every driveway in the country. For every car that had high CO_2 emissions, the price increase made the car unsaleable in most cases. For example, a brand-new Audi SUV, which already cost, say, €80,000 because of obscene levels of taxation already imposed on that vehicle (in Ireland we pay double tax on every new car, VAT and VRT, unlike in Europe where the only tax on cars is VAT, at a lower rate than ours), jumped in price by about €6,000 overnight because of its high emissions. This was simply an unrealistic price that the market couldn't bear. To further complicate the issue, high-emission cars also incurred increased road tax. So the net effect was stock values plummeted and hundreds of cars on forecourts in dealerships and in stock with distributors became unsaleable because they were now so expensive. The system broke down. It was the first of two major blows the industry had to endure.

The motor industry was also very reliant on credit, because in order to keep new cars in stock, you need finance advanced to pay for them before you can actually sell them. Typically, an average-sized dealership would stock about twenty-five new cars, so it would need about €1 million to finance that. When banks started collapsing all over the world, credit for depreciating cars was just not available.

But by the end of 2007 neither of these threats had materialised yet and we had sold nearly 3,000 units, cata-pulting our turnover to just under €34 million. Everything was working, but I knew we still had too many cars and we were still not banking any profit. Overheads were just too high, but I failed to act with any urgency to address this. If I had moved my arse then like I do now, I reckon all four dealerships could have survived. I don't know why I didn't. Maybe I was in denial, not wanting to admit that rapid expansion might not have been the best strategy. I had assumed that to borrow, develop and expand was the way to make a million. Hindsight tells me that this is not the case and that to increase your revenue you should stick to what you know and do best, perfect it until you are the best in your market, until your competition have no choice but to react and follow you, and then and only then should you consider a measured and controlled expansion, where you borrow no more than 40 per cent of the finance to do it.

I faced into 2008 feeling it would be a challenging year, but naively I still believed that I had everything under control. I could not have been more wrong. My father had been gone from the day-to-day operation for over seven years. I had worked hard to overcome any obstacles and make my own mark with our expansion. Just as I had everything in place, all ambition realised, and was knuckling down to make it start returning decent profit and working for me for the next decade, the Green Party pushed the detonate button for the car industry. Then, just four months later, Lehman Brothers collapsed. What happened over the next two years in Ireland destroyed some of the best businesses all over the country, caused many business owners and employees to take their own lives, resulted in many more fleeing the country and brought every bank in the country to its knees. It also stripped many older people who had worked all their lives and had pensions in the form of those 'safe-as-houses' blue-chip bank shares, of their life savings, which disappeared like sand through their hands.

A dark and dismal fear was about to seek out every self-employed man and woman in the country and when it found them it would possess them. I was no different, my time had come.

Chapter 8

Soft Landing My Arse

Blinding ignorance does mislead us. O! Wretched mortals, open your eyes!

Leonardo da Vinci

It was widely accepted in late 2007 that the Tiger would be tamed and that Ireland was about to enter an economic slow-down, the first to hit the country in seven years. Depending on their politics, economists had different views about the intensity of the slowdown but all agreed that there was a reversal of fortune on the way. The message from the government was still positive and we were told there would be a soft landing because there were two million people employed, the country had physically improved with new roads and amenities, and also that because our lifestyles had improved so much in the previous ten years, although things might get a little tougher than they had been, we were much better off in general. This 'soft landing' would mean a contraction in the economy, a bottoming out in a slow, measured way, not a crash.

This sort of rhetoric was getting massive national airtime and I was inclined to believe exactly what we were being told. By March 2008 a soft landing was still the talk of the day. If you believe the recent media claims that the political leaders of the time were fully aware of what was happening at Anglo-Irish Bank well before St Patrick's Day 2008, it looks like we were deliberately misled. Allegedly, within government and banking circles it was well known that Irish banks were going to face some sort of liquidity crisis before September 2008 and it was only a matter of how bad it would be. In May 2008 bank officials at one bank told me that their bank was going to face a 'moment of truth' in September. If officials in the south of the country knew this, how much information did the taoiseach, minister for finance, governor of the Central Bank and financial regulator have?

The bad news was that as a nation we were staring into an abyss, the good news was that we were blissfully ignorant of it at the time. If anyone who had invested in property or bank shares or both, like me, as well as expanding their business, could have seen what was coming, they would probably have chosen to drop their keys off at the local branch of the bank and disappear. I disagree with the position that nobody could have predicted the impact of the global economic meltdown. This situation was made worse in Ireland because of the failure to regulate and the banks lying about and covering up disastrous lending policies that led to things like Anglo borrowing from Permanent TSB and the 'golden circle' borrowing from Anglo to buy Anglo shares. It was only in early 2011 that the now infamous 'Blackrock stress tests' confirmed that the banks had not fully shown their hand when it came to their exposure to loans to the regular Joe Bloggs for personal loans, car loans, mortgages, etc.

If you look back at news reports during the period you can see what I call 'the cry of the lie':

> The €1.28 billion profit before taxation reported by AIB for the first half of 2008 represents a well balanced operating performance across our domestic and international businesses. This performance was achieved despite the adverse effect of slowing economies and difficult market conditions. It reflects the commitment of our people, deep customer relationships across geographically diverse franchises and a resilient risk management framework. All of this enables us to continue to operate effectively in the current challenging environment.
> Eugene Sheehy, Group Chief Executive AIB, August 2008[11]

Are we to believe that when a bank produces profits of €1.28 billion that they are not aware of their potential exposure? Why were the top people being so highly paid if they couldn't figure that one out? And if they had figured it out, why did they mislead their shareholders and the taxpayer?

---

11 AIB 2008 half-yearly financial report press release. See www.aib.ie/servlet/ ContentServer?pagename=AIB_Investor_Relations/AIB_Download/aib_d_ download&c=AIB_Download&cid=1213870630566&channel=IRFP

It was against this backdrop that I entered 2008 knowing that I had a few operational issues and challenges to contend with to start generating profit, but blissfully unaware of the financial meltdown looming with the financial partners that I was so dependent on. The following headlines tell the real truth, a truth that had I known I would have been able to adjust to, react to and prepare for. Within six months of issuing their interim annual report in 2008 stating that all was well, AIB had been bailed out by the government, as this headline demonstrates:

Recapitalisations of AIB, Bank of Ireland and EBS Building Society.

www.finance.gov.ie, 9 February 2009

Ten months later:

Lenihan says 'worst is over' as €4bn in cuts unveiled.

The Irish Times, December 2009

But that still wasn't the end:

Ireland to seek international bailout.

International Business Times, 21 November 2010[12]

---

12 www.ibtimes.com/articles/84136/20101121/ireland-to-seek-international-bailout.htm

Not having any of this information in the second half of 2007 but realising that the market had slowed and cash was getting tight, I was taking a far more active role in managing our cash flow, but by the time we reached St Patrick's Day in 2008 business had ground to a halt in all four dealerships. Footfall stopped. The message coming at the public from all angles was so negative people were scared. Our stock had hit levels of just under €7 million. The model mix was not good for any kind of dip in consumer confidence. We had 4x4s, SUVs and MPVs, all now much more difficult to sell. We still had funds from our retail finance deal with two banks. However, that system was set up in a time when cash flowed freely, and had worked brilliantly since 2004, but now it was starting to hinder our cash flow because consumer credit was not available, so we had no ability to service that agreement with our finance partners. We struggled away for about two months but the situation just got worse. There was real change in the country, the mood had shifted from confidence bordering on arrogance to absolute fear. The media was awash with economists taking on politicians like policemen trying to prove a crime.

I remember thinking 'you've got a problem here' a week before I was to take a summer holiday. Anne, the kids and I were due to head to the south of France in early June 2008 for a week. The business bank balances were so negative I dreaded the condition they would be in when I returned – not that I would have been able to stop the haemorrhage.

Nothing was selling and our cash was tied up in stock. I had to do something urgently, so I decided to fall back on our well-established and successful radio-advertising experience. I wrote a script and recorded it at a local radio station. I left town the day after I recorded the ad, having briefed my staff on how to handle the footfall – if it came.

Forty-eight hours later, while I was in France, the forecourt went nuts. We had massive footfall and the team struggled to cope at times. We sold in all four dealerships. Cash started to roll in again and the pressure was off for the time being, but the same old problem remained in that we weren't making any profit; in fact, some losses were being incurred. I thought that was inevitable because a 'correction' needed to take place after the introduction of the new VRT system. But I couldn't see a solution to the profitability problem and sensed that there would be more trouble ahead.

While in France I had time to reflect and decided that I needed to dump everything: houses, holiday home, cars, and I needed to do it fast. Although it was something I didn't really want to face, I knew deep down that we were heading down a road that had the potential to destroy us and I wasn't experienced enough to make the right decisions. I had never had to take on a bank other than in partnership and never really had to deal with stock and cash-flow problems of this magnitude. Now I was faced with doing both, for four businesses. The expansion that I had wanted so badly was threatening to bring about the downfall of the entire business.

I came up with a six-point plan to get the company through the tough times on the horizon:

1 Engage one of the 'big four' accountancy firms to ensure I received the best possible financial advice and to instil confidence in my financial partners.
2 Prepare a worst-case-scenario budget and cash-flow projection in consultation with accountants and then arrange to meet the financial partners with it – be proactive rather than reactive with them, and keep them in the loop.
3 Close the Chevrolet dealership and relocate the franchise back to the main showroom in Clonmel.
4 Reduce overheads by making at least ten redundancies.
5 Reduce stock to the value of €2 million over the next twelve months, at a loss if need be.
6 Sell any property that I could to reduce my personal borrowings.

I was determined. I believed I had the right team to get the business through and I would make all the right moves in the next twelve months. I returned home ready to attack the issues with vigour and implement my plan. I had come back to some cash coming in as a result of the ad I had done before I left. Within weeks I had also closed the Chevrolet showroom, made the redundancies, started the process of reducing our stock by selling it at a loss and placed five properties on the market for sale. I felt in control.

What I was not prepared for was a command from one of my financial partners that I meet them in Dublin for a review meeting not long after this. Having dealt with them cordially and successfully for the previous ten years I had never once been asked to meet for a review. With the help of my team I prepared thoroughly for this meeting – a business plan was written – and the intention was to take a proactive approach at the meeting, present the plan and leave with the bank onside. Unfortunately, they had a completely different idea of what the meeting was for. They controlled the meeting from the off, our business plan wasn't given a second look and they told us, very simply, that they wanted all their money back.

'How do you mean?' I asked, dumbfounded.

'We currently have exposure to your group, excluding new cars, of €2 million. We want it back,' they said.

What? I could not comprehend what I was hearing. I've misunderstood, haven't got it, I thought. They know the cash is all tied up in stock so I can't refund the cash.

'Why now?' I asked. 'We've had a successful system working between us for the last five years.'

'Everything is changing and we can't leave unsecured funding out there. Secure it or return it,' they said.

I left Dublin shell-shocked. I should have seen it coming but I hadn't. Secure the money how? The only remaining asset was the property at Davis Road.

That was only the first shock from a financial partner. Our second shock soon followed when our second financial partner wanted out after only six months. We had a very strong track record of selling retail car finance, but the endemic lack of credit in the Irish economy was hindering our ability to achieve the targets they had set us, and rather than ride it out with us they wanted to terminate immediately. When I met with them to discuss the issue I pointed out that our relationship had just started, that we were only months into it. I compared it to a 'young marriage and you want a divorce after our first fight!'

Despite my best efforts to persuade them, the bank took a hard line. There was no give in them whatsoever. They were insisting on getting their funds back and they wanted the money within a month. The figure was about €900,000 and the only security held was my personal guarantee. I was asked to meet the CEO in Dublin. I went to the meeting with my solicitor and we were met by three bank staff, including the CEO. The approach was aggressive and intimidating. I left the meeting shitting myself.

Driving home, all I could think about was banks. They had their hands around the neck of my businesses and it had all happened so fast. None of this was an issue at the start of 2008, but by the summer of that year I was in serious trouble with them all and our turnover was in free fall, so there was extreme pressure coming from all sides. It felt as though it had all happened overnight and I didn't understand it. Why were they all so urgent and irrational about getting the money back without giving us a chance to trade our way out of this? Why was my home being threatened? I spent the next twelve hours in a state of blind panic bordering on hysteria. Fear had utterly gripped me and that was the evening I found myself picturing my own funeral and deciding it was time to fight back.

The reason for their urgency became clear in the coming months as the banking crisis unfolded. During the good times being financed by a number of banks gives each one of them more confidence in your business – it is like they are validating each other's investment. When the opposite happens, however, the effects are devastating, as one by one they withdraw their support and it all falls apart like a house of cards. My reality was changing. My optimistic view of life was ebbing away, things that would normally lift my spirits were becoming irrelevant and my sleep pattern was all over the place. I was extremely worried. Owning a business that owed millions to three different banks was terrifying and I felt that my entire family was looking at me and asking, 'How are you going to fix this?'

For days after those meetings I was punch-drunk. I had long conversations with trusted colleagues, my father and Anne. My father was supportive but detached – he didn't have the same exposure to personal guarantees as I did. I knew I had to do something but had no idea what and I was panicking. My bank shares were in serious trouble now, too, and the motor industry was effectively shut down.

I had wanted the big business, I had borrowed the money, I had thrust out my chest for three years, talking about how good we were. I should have been better at managing it. I should have ensured that I had all the relevant and accurate information and I should have made certain that any decisions I took were fully informed. I did not.

I had foolishly agreed to service one of my debts by making payments of €50,000 per month. This was proving impossible to do with car sales at an all-time low, and the banks were utterly merciless. There were constant phone calls, and threatening letters arrived at my home. They left me under no illusion about what they would do if the debt was not serviced. If a receiver was appointed in a worst-case scenario I would lose one of my franchises and that would effectively close two dealerships instantly. I consulted with my accountants and decided to fight the issue, to try to persuade them to restructure the debt so that I would have a fighting chance of servicing it. A new business plan would be written and I'd go back to both banks and make a more substantial presentation, presented by a professional team. My logic was that the banks would have more confidence if they knew that I was receiving professional advice.

It took €35,000 and three months to compile the documents. When the plan was ready I arranged separate meetings with both banks in Dublin, and the top-brass accountants flew from Cork to present the plan with me. What an anti-climax. Both banks said that the business plan, especially the cash-flow projections, were 'light'. My presentation team had failed to inspire or impress either bank. I was devastated. Hadn't I done the right thing? I had hired this team and certainly paid well for their advice, so I was trusting in them to at least deliver data that was at the very least substantial enough to get the banks' attention. How could they have made a presentation that the bank considered to be light on relevant information?

Despite three months' hard work and huge expense, nothing had changed except my bank balance. The pressure was now intense from all my financial partners and business was a hundred times worse than it had been before my holiday to France four months earlier. One financial partner was particularly immovable and had no interest in listening to any proposals. They had made their decision – repay all the money or give them security for it. The other, at least, was accepting monthly instalments. After consultation with those around me it was decided to concentrate first on clearing the balance owed by our main dealership at Davis Road. Once that was achieved we would move onto the other dealerships.

The very real and dramatic effects of the new VRT system continued to destroy the value of used cars, especially cars that had been registered in 2007 or 2008. These cars were relatively new and of high value, and we were carrying significant levels of them spread across the group. On top of this the business had commitments to buy back rental cars in the summer of 2008. Part of our business had been to engage in the process of selling high volumes of cars to leasing and rental companies and this had been a very successful side of our business for about ten years. Clearly, the values of these fleets would now be destroyed. The devaluation issue existed with cars that were registered in 2007 that were due to be returned in the summer of 2008 and those registered in the first two months of 2008 that were due back in late 2008. The organisation had exposure on these cars of around €850,000. Once these cars arrived back to the dealerships on their predetermined date they needed to be paid for and so the business would incur heavy losses on them as they were now worth less than they had been bought for because of the new taxation changes. Receiving these cars back into stock was like a plane flying on three engines taking on more passengers and luggage while at the same time turning off the third engine.

Our total stock of vehicles was at this time in excess of €7 million, and we still had to pay for a large proportion of that stock. We were in big trouble. We needed time, patience and a long-term view to get out of this mess, but we were dealing with panicking banks. Had they been calmer and taken a long-term view we all would have emerged in a better condition. I was trying to make monthly payments of €50,000 while also signing away the last bit of equity that we had, in the property at Davis Road (with my father's OK), to offer the security that one of the banks required, while my business was in absolute free fall. I started to dump stock like toxic bank shares just to lodge money. This was a huge mistake. It has become clear to me that if you are being pressured into giving or improving your security position with the bank it is better to just say no. You need to be as ruthless as the banks – your survival is at stake. Tell them to get in line. Sit on your working capital and only pay them a little at a time – whatever you can realistically afford. Do not be coerced into writing a 'panic cheque' if you are pressured either verbally or in writing. Get tough now, if you still can.

Banks all over the world were struggling, but in Ireland that struggle was acute and so bank share values plummeted. Another big problem for me was my AIB shares. My experiment with CFDs was now becoming a serious liability. I had bought shares at around €18 per share, but by now their worth had crashed to €10 per share. I was advised that if I could afford to I should hold on, but if I could not I should sell. I cashed in at about €9 per share. It was a painful loss but in fact I had a lucky escape. Within months, the shares were worth twenty-four cent. I lost €365,000. The devaluation of the bank shares was devastating for me and thousands of others, many of whom had invested their life savings in 'blue chip' bank shares and intended to retire on the strength of it, never imagining such a disaster was even possible.

It's on public record that the then Taoiseach Brian Cowen received a phone call from Seán Fitzpatrick, the then chairman of Anglo-Irish Bank, while he was visiting Asia on an official St Patrick's Day visit in 2008. They discussed both banking and CFD issues (at the time businessman Seán Quinn had acquired nearly 30 per cent of Anglo-Irish Bank through the use of CFDs) that would soon become public knowledge and cause irreversible damage not only to Anglo but to the entire banking sector. A statement from the Department of the Taoiseach in January 2011 confirmed that Brian Cowen then contacted the governor of the Central Bank and the financial regulator asking them to investigate Fitzpatrick's revelations.[13] If all of the parties who could have called a halt and suspended CFD trading or at least put the problems on public record were aware of what was going on as far back as March 2008, what the bloody hell was I, and so many others, doing dealing in bank shares right into 2009? It was, in my opinion, utterly negligent to keep silent. People were dealing in a controlled, rotten market. How will the over-sixty-fives recover from their share losses? Younger people may be able to go on and try to make money again in the future. The entire system was fixed, anti-competitive and completely underhand.

The year 2008 was turning out to be one of the most difficult periods of my life, but it was a story that was still evolving,

13 www.taoiseach.gov.ie/eng/Government_Press_Office/Taoiseach's_Press_Releases_2011/Statement_by_the_Taoiseach_Mr_Brian_Cowen_T_D_in_relation_to_Sean_Fitzpatrick_Book.html

with new twists and turns emerging all the time. By summertime I believed that we were in a horrible downturn and that the difficulties we were experiencing were unique to my company. Now I realise that most businesses, no matter how big or small, liquid or not, were affected and that for companies all over Ireland cash flow had become the single biggest issue. It was more than just a slowdown, it was global, it was toxic. Even banks ran out of cash. Employers sat in offices in mid-2008 making decisions without the full knowledge of what was really happening, feeling alone and in the dark, and hoping that what was happening to their business would sort itself out over the next twelve months. All we could do was do our best to remain solvent and try to trade our way out. It had to be business as usual insofar as was possible.

In late 2008 I approached Kia Ireland seeking a business relationship. I wanted our brand to become the new franchise holder for Kia in south Tipperary and they wanted to locate the franchise in our now vacant Chevrolet showroom. The brand was up and coming. Future Kia product that was due to be launched over the next five years was sensational. I liked their approach, it was honest and to the point. There were no major demands. I thought that taking on the Kia franchise would enhance our cash flow, so I accepted and within eight weeks we were appointed. For a while it was business as usual, but we were forced to relocate the Kia franchise to our main showroom six months later as it quickly became clear that it wasn't profitable as a stand-alone franchise given the market conditions. So we closed the old Daewoo showroom once and for all.

Then the old thorny issue of succession in the business resurfaced, because my father was having his own cash-flow problems – access to credit had been cut off for everyone, so Dad needed to take cash out of his business and this was adding to my problems. We had a very difficult meeting at my office to try to find a solution that would work for me, the business and my father. After months of discussions and taking advice we agreed to sign a share-offer agreement that would be mutually beneficial, giving my brother and I the power to trigger the transfer of ownership at a time that would suit us and giving my father financial security. We signed the agreement during Christmas week 2008. When my father signed it effectively ended his ownership of the company. Six days later my parents celebrated Christmas Day with Anne and myself. It was our turn to host them. It was very, very difficult for all concerned. Succession in family business is emotive and will be painful if not planned, managed and prepared for. In our case, succession of both ownership and day-to-day control came at a huge emotional cost.

I had begun to feel the physical effects of the pressure I was under by the start of September. By now we were haemorrhaging cash. We were losing over €100,000 every month. I had already made some cuts but now I needed to aggressively attack our overheads. I sat down with my core team to review the functionality of our day-to-day operations. More redundancies would be needed. Within days we announced a wave of redundancies and I honestly believed that we would only need to seek redundancies once. Months later we needed to do another round, followed by still more a few months after that. It was traumatic for all concerned. Every penny we spent was reviewed. Every heading in our profit-and-loss account was scrutinised. I was touched and so appreciative when some staff came to me and offered to take salary reductions. I knew these people understood the urgency and reality of our situation and would go the distance.

At reviews with both banks we were complimented on being ahead of many with our approach. They told us that some companies were in denial, believing that the downturn wouldn't be as bad as first reported or that they wouldn't be affected by it. Up to that point we had only ever needed to recruit, we had only known growth and there was real pain in making redundancies. We knew that families were depending on us and we hated every second of it, but the organisation's survival was at stake. Some days we would have to call in eight or nine people and break the news. There were tears, real sympathy and a real sense of doom around the dealerships. Everybody was on the alert.

I had to rationalise it to myself just to cope, telling myself it was their family or mine. I would look at myself in the mirror in the morning, after letting ten people go the day before, and wonder how I did it. I felt utterly disappointed in myself. It wasn't like a human-resources department in a big company – cold and impersonal. It was the owner talking to people I knew, who I had hired, who lived around the corner, on a one-to-one basis. Their kids went to the same school as mine. I repeatedly told myself that the people I had to make redundant would get a redundancy payment and social-welfare payments on some level, but as a proprietary director of a company if my business failed and I was out of a job and had no income I'd get nothing. Over the months that followed, my father and I and many like us would pump every penny we had into the company to keep it going. If it failed I was out on the street without a penny. I think that's wrong, discourages entrepreneurship and is discriminatory. I pay taxes like everybody else and would be willing to pay personal PRSI if it meant that I, too, could be looked after by the state if my business failed, so why is there no support for the self-employed if everything goes belly up?

This was a world I was not used to. It was a world that was becoming very scary. Trying to stay focused enough to make the right decisions became a challenge. We were selling cars at big losses. For every ten cars sold we lost about €30,000. This wasn't because of the economic slowdown. The chickens had come home to roost. The real culprits were the new VRT system, combined with dealerships becoming whipping boys for distribution companies who insisted that market share for their product was increased, resulting in overtrading. We simply had too many cars in stock and this was tying up our cash. Supply was much greater than demand and it had been like that for about four years.

By late 2008 I was really starting to fear the worst. Could I lose the business? I was beginning to think it would happen. The big hit came late in the year when Lehman Brothers went under. When that happened the world changed irreparably. The pressure mounted and there was no escaping the fear. It was everywhere.

A few days later I felt like I couldn't cope any longer and thought I was going to break down in tears, so I just walked out of my office, didn't speak to anybody, got in my car, left my mobile phone behind and drove. I kept driving until the front wheels of the car literally touched the salt water of the ocean. I had driven in a straight line for about eighty miles to a place called The Point, which is a section of beach on the east coast, near Rosslare. It was wintertime and cold, but it was silent. I was on my own there. I stopped the car and put the driver's seat back and fell asleep to the sound of the ocean. I was exhausted.

About an hour later I woke up. I got out and walked for about a mile. I found a great big rock and sat down on it to consider my options. I sat there and thought: 'What do I need to do to fix this?' I needed this space and time to consider my next move. Between that time on the beach and my slow drive home I figured out what I needed to do. I would need to make more redundancies and instil absolute confidence in the two banks that were supporting me. I also needed to streamline our day-to-day procedures to make the running of the company easier.

I drove home from Rosslare on the day that banks across the world went bust. Absolute meltdown occurred, the likes of which I suspect, or rather hope, we'll never see again. As the day unfolded and the media reported the true extent and potential fallout of what was happening, it became very clear to me that I would be very, very lucky if my business survived this. The next three or four months would doubtless decide our fate. I was terrified that the business would fail. Why wouldn't it? Banks were chasing us, turnover was down 50 per cent, the property was in negative equity and no one would buy it anyway. This was not a soft landing, it was a crash and burn.

We managed to continue our monthly payments but it was hurting, as were the losses on stock sales. We continued to reduce stock and continued to reduce staff numbers and overheads. October to December in the car industry is generally a difficult period, but those three months in 2008 were horrific. We made it to the end of the year having lost a fortune.

There was a mantra going about at this point that if a business could survive 2009 it would survive the recession. The good times were well and truly over, and by the end of 2008 I'd have been delighted with the prospect of owning a solid business rather than a multi-franchise motor group. In twelve short months our industry had been turned on its head because of government policy and the banking crisis. Despite this I had good reason to think that the worst was over – we had cut our overheads by 50 per cent, I had a good feeling about the Kia franchise and what it would produce, we were meeting our repayments to the first financial partner, were holding the second at bay because they now had the security they required and I had dealt with the thorny succession issue once and for all. Perhaps we had done enough in time.

The year 2009 was just around the corner. It would bring us to the edge of a cliff.

Chapter 9

Shepherd's Pie

You have brains in your head.
You have feet in your shoes.
You can steer yourself in any direction you choose.
You're on your own.
And you know what you know.
You are the guy who'll decide where to go.

Dr Seuss, *Oh, the Places You'll Go!*

Ireland Inc. had suffered greatly over the year that was 2008 and for many business owners it was about picking up the pieces as they began 2009. We began the new year accepting that we were in a full-blown recession as opposed to how we entered 2008, thinking that some form of slowdown was imminent. All sorts of businesses were suffering but buying a new car was simply not on the agenda – in fact it was almost considered vulgar to own a new car during 2009. A new car might suggest that you were exempt from the slowdown when thousands were losing their jobs.

There was no sign of any sort of recovery on the horizon for our business. We continued to reduce our stock and continued to incur significant losses. We were still under scrutiny from the banks. Our monthly payment of €50,000 was hurting more and more every month. Looking at the bank accounts depressed me because we were so overdrawn.

Within the first few months of 2009 there was an increase in the suicide rate around the country and this trend continued into 2010.[14] Clonmel was not spared from this brutal reality. People were under enormous pressure. On the day of one of those local tragic occurrences, I received a phone call from a bank manager asking me if I was OK. He said it was 'important to ask the question'. It was a sincere phone call but it demonstrated the gravity of the situation that business owners were in with their financial partners. Maybe it demonstrated some humanity amongst all the ruthlessness or maybe he had been instructed to call. Either way, it was a bizarre conversation. Newspapers carried frequent stories about developers, farmers, shop owners, people from all walks of life resorting to suicide, buckling under the immense pressure. People running their own businesses were terrified that they might not have the cash reserves or the skill to navigate their way out of the disaster they found themselves in.

---

14 National Office for Suicide Prevention Annual Report 2009, accessible at www.nosp.ie.

I realised very early in the year that I didn't have the working capital to keep all four dealerships open. I was especially worried about Kilkenny because it was the newest dealership and hadn't yet built up a solid customer base. I needed to discuss the issue with the bank that had financed the premises, and phoned on a Tuesday morning. Later that day senior bank officials from that bank had me in an office where we sat and talked until late into the evening about the pros and cons of closing. They talked me out of it. My intention was to close but they strongly advised against that, telling me to hang on and see if the economy, or at least the car business, would turn. I took their advice and held off on my decision, but I was amazed at their reaction and I honestly believe that they had no idea how serious things were or how the business worked – or rather, wasn't working.

From this I learned another valuable lesson: do not discuss strategy with banks. If I had not taken their advice I would have closed Kilkenny quickly and saved considerable money. For them to actively talk me out of a decision that critical for the long-term survival of our company is completely bizarre. Were they talking me out of closing to avoid having an impaired loan appearing on their system? I don't know, but either way it was the wrong decision.

Six months later I finally pulled the plug. GBM Cityside in Kilkenny had failed. It was a difficult decision to take and was made on the basis that I wanted to protect what I had in Clonmel rather than risk the lot. I was not afraid to make a tough decision and live with the consequences. I notified the staff and Renault. My father, the bank, Renault and many others disagreed with the decision, but my gut told me it was the right thing to do and I stuck to my guns. Our other distributors then began to get nervous as they were obviously having their own problems and were now worried that their dealer network could collapse, increasing their exposure to bad debt, too.

Closing any part of a business in a small town or city attracts public attention. We wanted people to know that it was our decision not the bank's, and that anyone who had become a customer of ours in the two years we had traded in Kilkenny was welcome to visit our Renault dealership in Clonmel if their car needed any work. Closing the Kilkenny business reduced our monthly overheads considerably. I felt that this decision, together with the reductions in overheads made in 2008, would mean that I could focus all of my attention on the three remaining dealerships in Clonmel. I was wrong.

I had truly believed that sales couldn't get any worse than in 2008, but trading conditions continued to worsen and now our combined overdrafts exceeded €1.3 million. I was fighting a losing battle. I just could not control our cash flow. I had created a gigantic creature that soaked up cash. While I had the sympathy and support of my brother and my core team, as the managing director ultimately it was my responsibility to try to sort things out. I imagine that I wasn't alone in feeling that way across the country, as many other business owners must have been sharing the experience. My world had become focused on only one thing – cash. Between the banks, Revenue, creditors and our distributors I was utterly consumed, moving from one crisis to another on a daily basis. It felt like we were under constant attack from the banks in all aspects of the business – it was like they knew something we didn't, which, as we subsequently found out, they did. They wanted so many reports. We were already struggling with the onslaught of the recession and even if we had had time to produce all the reports they asked for, the outlook changed daily. Each bank became utterly obsessed with the other banks we were dealing with, as though each one was afraid that they were the only bank not getting paid. They were relentless.

My home life suffered and I felt pressure everywhere I turned. I cannot describe the feeling that you are about to fail. This was the family business. It was in my care, was my responsibility – at my insistence. Was I about to lose it? God, I had been such a loudmouth in the press over the five years that I had been expanding. So many people would like to see me taken down a peg. I began to experience a spiralling sense of despair and desperation. What would my kids think, how would I explain it to them? How would I pay the wages tomorrow, what about that letter from Revenue on my desk? I constantly felt nauseous, was trying to force sleep that wouldn't come, and was making myself sick with worry. A typical night would find me staring at the ceiling at 3 a.m. with a knot in my stomach that deprived me of appetite and energy. I'd just start to drift off and feel that false sense of security that occurs between falling asleep and waking and then WHAM – THE BANK and I'm wide awake again.

It was slow torture. By day I could not get warm. It was a remarkably cold winter and everything seems more miserable in the cold and wet. Because I couldn't eat or sleep I began to lose weight – just a few pounds at first, but then enough that people began remarking that I was looking thin. I tried to eat but couldn't taste food and anyway, it turned my stomach. I couldn't get cash out of my mind, just couldn't think of anything else. Driving my car, standing in a queue, even talking to people, I was just staring at them with a hapless smile, not hearing a word. When I was walking down the street, spending time with my family, I was there in body but my mind was always elsewhere – every minute of every day, from first thing in the morning to last thing at night. My team could see that my head was down and they were worried about me, but they must have been very worried for their own livelihoods, too, seeing my body language.

I had taken every cent that I owned privately and sunk it into the company to try to keep everything afloat. Now I was personally broke, too, and the business was no better off. I was so focused on my business problems that I hadn't been a dad or a husband for months, and even though I knew that and felt guilty about it, the stress I was feeling came out at home and there were plenty of rows. This only compounded my stress levels. Anne was incredibly patient but pleaded with me to end the cycle of misery any way I could. Easier said than done.

A typical day at the office was like a battle. I was jaded. Lonely. Terrified. It has been like that for self-employed people in Ireland for three years now. Arrears in rent, arrears with Revenue who are ramping up the intensity of their demand letters, no finance available from banks, no sales, only bad news from the media – will they ever stop talking about the banks and recession? What do you do, where do you go to for advice, who can help? It's unknown territory for most of us. My life had become all about firefighting. Every hour of every day was dominated by banks or cash. We were selling nothing, the phone wasn't ringing, the showroom was deathly silent. As I became more and more gripped by the fear of what could happen I drifted further inside myself and removed myself from the day-to-day operation of the business. My staff, junior and senior, were on their own now. No one could get near me. I was in lockdown.

My working life became a sixteen-hour-day, seven-days-a-week, round-the-clock effort. We were losing hundreds of thousands of euro monthly. I was battling three banks, dealing with a new regime and a disgruntled Renault after closing Kilkenny, while simultaneously trying to reshape our business model and making redundancies. All this before I even thought about the €7 million worth of stock that wasn't selling. I would wake up after another sleepless night, reach over the side of my bed and pick up the file or computer that I left there six hours earlier. Within eight minutes of waking I was working. I'd leave for the office early, then get home around 8 p.m., say hello to the kids and work again until midnight. Saturdays and Sundays were consumed with the backlog of operational issues and compiling reports and data for the banks. My kids would complain that I was always working. Guilt would set in. I was trapped in a vicious circle where I felt damned if I did and damned if I didn't. It felt like a life sentence.

My goal was to keep my creditors and the banks at bay in the hope that we could sell some stock, but I knew that we would need more financial support to get us through. I could prove to the banks that I was taking radical action to get our losses under control, and they acknowledged this. One bank agreed that in all functional companies there would come a point when rock bottom would be reached, when working capital ran out having supported losses, but the losses had stopped and stocks were reducing. Since mid-2008 we had reduced our stock from a value of €6.7 million to €1.2 million, incurring huge losses, but at least we had reached the end of that cycle. So I was now in a position, based on the bank's own criteria, to apply for funding for working capital.

The bank told me that they 'hope to get it over the line but it will be difficult'. The individual I was dealing with said that he felt that the bank had a 'moral responsibility' to assist. Wow. This was someone who obviously felt uncomfortable with how his employer had conducted business over the boom years. My plan was to try to get all the banks involved to support us by advancing new working-capital facilities so that each would take comfort from the other's involvement and go back to their credit committee to sell the application. Credit committees in banks had control of lending decisions at this point. They were a difficult breed to get around for even the best lending manager.

I wanted to get the banks talking to each other, which would not be an easy thing to achieve. It was July 2009 and we needed emergency funds, so the burning question was how quickly could I get all of them in a room together, and then how quickly could I get them to run the application up the line to their credit committees. I quickly learned that banks do not move at speed. By the time you get a decision, sign offer letters, deal with securities and legals, months can pass. That time delay only serves to worsen cash-flow positions, which ultimately creates an even more negative position for both the business owner and the bank. It was October before I could get all the relevant parties to agree to meet in Clonmel and that was an achievement in itself. It was a very difficult meeting, ultimately resulting in one bank supporting us and one bank pulling out at the last minute. Very difficult questions were asked of me and my ability – I should have asked them the same questions!

Once NAMA came into existence, the banks, which had been irrational up to now, became completely dysfunctional, gripped by their own fear. When I lodged funds from my personal account to the company account, from one bank to another, I got a call the next day from the company's bank asking why I had lodged the money and asking where I got it. If I wrote a cheque to myself and tried to cash it I would receive a call and be asked why was I paying myself. Paranoia, indecision and fear were rife in the banking sector. We were looking at up to a six-month wait for a decision after the Clonmel meeting and I wasn't sure that we would survive that long. I stopped paying anything that didn't directly result in keeping the door open and the lights on, and even then I only paid the minimum – I had to, our survival was at stake. Stock continued to move slowly and consistently, but the losses kept coming. People were buying used cars, but because of the new VRT system we had to sell them at a price lower than cost. If that system had not been introduced I think we could have coped with the downturn because at least any stock we managed to sell would have been at a profit. I wonder how different our business would look but for that particular piece of legislation. It was a real killer.

In 2009 Renault announced that a new distribution model would be introduced in Ireland. How would this affect us? Time would tell, but it was clear to me that Renault would not suffer fools gladly. By now, we were in pure survival mode. It was absolutely exhausting. Every day was a battle for survival. Every time the phone rang it was a bank or a creditor or another problem. There was no reprieve. We made more redundancies. From the first redundancies made in September 2008 to the last round in November 2009 we ended up letting forty people in total go, reducing staff numbers from fifty-three to thirteen. The country itself was in financial trouble and the outlook was incredibly bleak. Unemployment was heading for 12 per cent (it had reached 14 per cent by the time of writing this), the banks were in a state of chaos, house prices were in free fall, the government was preparing its second emergency budget of the year and as a people the Irish were losing confidence rapidly in their political leaders.

Nobody was thinking about buying cars. From a high of over 200,000 new cars bought in the year 2000, just about 55,000 were bought in 2009. Sales were back at 1988 levels but mortgage repayments and overhead levels were very much those of 2009. I was on the brink. I felt like I just couldn't carry the load anymore. I still find it difficult to describe what it was like to be in charge, believing that we were heading for a total crash and not having a clue how to prevent it and turn the ship around.

It had been eighteen months since that holiday in France when I had decided to offload as many buildings and as much stock as possible and began my fight by telling the bank not to call me. It was nearly twelve months since Lehman's went under and during that time Ireland had discovered that its financial system was so flawed that it ran the risk of bankrupting a country that had been in an economic boom for twenty years. So many businesses were suffering the fallout of this, and countless employers like me were battling to save their businesses under pressure so intense that life had become unbearable.

Despite my earlier conviction, I had reached the stage where I no longer wanted to fight the battle. I wanted to throw in the towel. I was hugely indecisive, constantly changing my mind. I was so irritable that even the people closest to me wondered if I could cope. I just wanted to stay in bed. Every day I longed for it to get to the point at night when it was 11 p.m. and I could put my head down. I didn't want to talk to anyone. I talked so much during the day that I felt like I had literally run out of words and lost the ability to speak when I got home in the evening. I was so exhausted that I could not engage with my family. I was miles away. If there was a moment of calm at the office I was sure that the next crisis was just around the corner. I couldn't relax and couldn't remember what downtime even felt like.

Inevitably, Anne's patience ran out. She was resentful of the expansion, believing that it was the cause of all our problems, and felt that had I not pushed for expansion as I had then we wouldn't have been suffering as badly. Her own business was suffering, too, she was fatigued and desperately worried about me, and in the heat of a desperate argument she urged me to walk away. But everything we had had gone into the company. We wouldn't be able to claim any assistance from the state and if I was to walk away, shut everything down and liquidate, we would be left with absolutely nothing. The banks would be left trying to recover over €11 million so their reaction would be ferocious and we'd have new battles to fight. This was the big conundrum: do you hang on, can you hang on, have you the mental strength? Or do you say fuck it, life is too short and walk out on it all, but in doing so, jump from the frying pan into the fire?

During one of our many late-night arguments I promised that I would do everything I could to get our family unit back to some normality. I vividly remember making that promise. I really wanted to deliver. Life had become so negative and dour that it was having a very adverse effect on our relationship. I was determined to achieve a more balanced lifestyle but I knew that it would take some time. My priority now was to protect our family home and to make sure that we would be OK personally if the business collapsed.

On a winter's evening in November 2009 I pulled up at my house. It was pitch dark outside. I felt so emotional, broken and defeated. I was blaming myself for what had happened, berating myself that I was the only one responsible for the mess I found myself in. I had spent five years fighting my father for control, four years building my dream and over two years trying to survive. It was affecting my health, my relationship, my kids, my family and my staff. That black evening, sitting in my car outside my house at around 8 p.m., was my lowest point. I got out of the car, opened the front door and walked into a warm kitchen. Anne was there, and George and Emily were sitting at the kitchen table eating a dinner of steaming shepherd's pie and watching cartoons. I wanted to break down and cry. I wanted to be free of banks, business, cars and customers. I wanted to be with Anne and the kids and relax. I can't describe the torture I was feeling at that moment. I walked to the table and said hi to the kids. They looked up at me and said, 'Hi Dad', with warm smiles, delighted to see me. Unconditional love and faith beamed from their faces and with it they had sent a message that only I could receive. It said we love you, we're proud of you and we trust you completely.

Snap!

A sense of urgency came over me, a moment of clarity where I thought to myself, 'Hey, asshole, wake up, you've got to get out there and find tomorrow's shepherd's pie. This is your problem so fix it whatever way you have to. This is war. Fight hard, dirty if you have to, and look on the bright side. If you win you win and if you lose you can walk away knowing you tried everything.'

The decision was made. I got up the next morning and while the fears and anxiety were still there I was feeling ready for the fight. I decided to use the image of my kids eating dinner at the kitchen table to give me strength every time the pressure felt like too much.

After my 'shepherd's pie moment' I believed that the real fight was only just beginning and that I would need a new approach, a new outlook. I had read a book called *The Secret* months earlier and found myself revisiting it the day after the shepherd's pie moment. I had found the book's premise interesting – that you can determine your future with the power of positive thinking – but hadn't thought much more about it. Now seemed like a good time to try the approach as I desperately needed to change something in order to win this battle. I chose to control my fear and believe that I could see this through.

I began training my mind this way, not just paying lip service to an idea but really believing that there would be a positive outcome and specifying in writing what I believed would happen – what I needed to happen. Whatever the outcome then I would accept it. Fuck anyone who wanted me to fail and fuck being mortified by any potential failure.

I had made the decision that I would give it everything in one final push for survival. I felt a new sense of urgency and ruthlessness, became decisive, took action and started to feel like I was in control again, could cope. As time passed I also felt a physical change occur as my body got used to the long hours which I had accepted would become my reality, and my mind got to grips with the fear. It wasn't all plain sailing – there were still days I felt hopeless and defeated and others where I felt overjoyed because we sold a car and had a cash inflow, but I had decided to own the emotions rather than allow them to own me. My weekend was made if I arrived home on a Friday night having made a lodgement that would get us to the middle of the following week. My weekend was ruined if I knew that I had nothing in the bank for Monday.

I developed a daily routine where I wouldn't look at the bank balance until about 1 p.m. because any cash that was due would have hit the account by then and there would be very little movement thereafter. Close scrutiny of the statements helped me to learn the system. An overdrawn balance at 10 a.m. on a Tuesday would not have to be dealt with until 4 p.m. on Wednesday. I was working about twenty-seven hours behind the bank. I learned to deal with today's issues today. Everything in my mind was compartmentalised – there was no point dealing with issues that were on the horizon, that *might* happen, when there was plenty to deal with today. If a creditor was looking for money I'd agree to pay in three days' time after 4 p.m. because the banks were closed. I knew the cheque would be presented for payment the next day which wouldn't be an issue for me until another day later, just before 4 p.m. I managed to get on average an extra week from each creditor by working this system. That was an extra week having already had 120 days' credit. Of course I was having the same problems everyone was having getting paid by my customers and debtors. Nobody was paying anybody because cash was so tight. I battled every day of every week so that we could hang on.

While this battle for survival went on I was intolerant of anything that wasn't part of it. I was so focused that I couldn't engage in anything else. I moved at speed. There was no room for procrastination. I barely stopped to answer questions from staff and I didn't suffer fools gladly. I was a nightmare for those close to me at work. I pushed people very hard and demanded long, intense days. I needed mental toughness from everybody. My core team found it particularly difficult as they had to deal with all of this while watching their friends and colleagues being made redundant. The atmosphere was dreadful. There were tears, arguments, difficult decisions to be made and someone had to make them – me. I hated every second of it and could just about function. I still wasn't sleeping properly and didn't feel at all energised if I managed a few hours.

I just wanted to be left alone to get on with things. The idea that somebody wanted or needed something from me, even one of my kids asking me for something, was overwhelming. One day merged into the next. It was total mental exhaustion, but this time I was driven, determined not to let those bastards bring me down. I was now managing every aspect of my company. It was like I had put my arms around it to protect it. Every decision no matter what size was made by me and me alone. I had a firm grip on the business but still wasn't making money, getting creative or coming up with new ideas. I still wasn't driving the business. I knew that I needed to get an injection of cash, and if I got it I believed that survival was possible. If our application for working capital was rejected, though, it was all over.

Months had slipped by since we made the application and we had battled for every day. Every excuse under the sun was given for the lack of progress on a decision, but finally I received a phone call in December 2009, six months later, informing me that I would have the decision by 4 p.m. that evening. I headed home to receive the call there, with Anne and the kids with me, because this would be make or break. Thankfully the loan was approved, but with lots of conditions and at a huge emotional and financial cost in that all assets (bar our family homes) were now cross-charged.[15] I had no choice but to accept the conditions and so on Christmas Eve signed the paperwork. This gave us some breathing space but we were going to have significantly less cash with which to try to run two separate, large premises – Nissan and Kia at Davis Road and Renault at GBM. It was going to be incredibly difficult. The plan was to get the cash and go back to basics come January. Nissan had one or two consistently big sellers but the real winner for 2010 would surely be Renault, because their marketing strategy and new suite of cars would be sure-fire successes. The new cars and

15 A cross charge over assets is where a lender holds an asset or assets as security against a particular loan. For example, take a loan of €1 million with four assets being held as security by the lender. Each asset will have a registered charge applied by the lender against the loan, therefore one loan might have four assets held by one registered charge.

marketing strategy had invigorated the dealer network and we believed that we could make some profit at last.

Despite all the redundancies that had been made, the strength, loyalty and commitment of my core team, including my brother Brian, never waned. I relied on them heavily and they tolerated my irritability over and above the call of duty. I was unbearable to be around, I fought with everybody because I had become programmed to fight. A core team that can see what you are trying to achieve, who trust you and can in return be trusted and who have insight, patience, wisdom and experience is absolutely invaluable.

Eight months earlier, in March 2009, I had travelled to Manchester with Brian and a core member of staff to do some reconnaissance work on understanding the trade in the UK and to establish some contacts. We were thinking of importing quality used cars. Although over the last couple of years we had reduced our stocks significantly to raise cash, we anticipated that in future years there would be an increased demand for used cars in Ireland and wanted to see what the British dealerships were doing so that we could learn from them to improve our own dealership. We hired a UK-based consultant to open doors for us and to educate us. We started to understand car values in the UK and eased into importing the cars.

We got a few wrong at first but before long we found our feet. We believed that there would be a shortage of used cars in Ireland in 2010 and 2011 because so few people were trading in to buy new cars. If only 55,000 cars had been sold in 2009 then there would only be 55,000 two-year-old cars in 2011 and how many of them would be available to buy? We wanted to get ahead of the competition. Sterling was also fragile, so benefitting from the exchange rate also made it worthwhile. That trip would prove instrumental to our recovery although we had no idea of just how important it would be at the time.

The other great incentive that emerged in 2009 was a decision by the Revenue Commissioners to change VAT administration in the motor industry from a VATable used-car system to a marginal VAT system, called the VAT Margin Scheme. The transition to this new system allowed motor dealers to retain a percentage of their normal VAT returns as a once-off rebate, effectively reducing their VAT bill and improving profitability and cash flow. This good news was topped off by the announcement that the government would introduce a new scrappage scheme, allowing people to claim a rebate of up to €1,500 from the government for trading in an old banger.

As we approached 2010 we had some fresh funding, new models to sell from all distributors, a franchise in Renault that we believed was about to set records in the country, the new VAT Margin Scheme and the scrappage scheme. Having been to hell and back in 2009, there was finally reason to be positive. However, by the end of the year we were also having to face a very public liquidation, having closed dealerships. Failure to do so could have resulted in the debt moving from the limited company to the directors personally and I had no choice legally. This was to have unforeseen consequences.

It was mid-December 2009 and the progress we were making and how much we were looking forward to 2010 and getting stuck into our recovery now seemed pointless. Liquidation is very public. When you liquidate a company you must run small advertisements in newspapers informing all creditors. I was told that we were legally obliged to advertise a creditors' meeting within fourteen days of the ads appearing. We were going to have to do it and I would have to consult with distributors and other partners and staff to give them the whole story, as that sort of news coming out without all of the background information could be devastating. A double liquidation. Jesus, most people do it only once. I was going to have the first liquidation at 11.30 a.m. on 28 January 2010 with the second at 1 p.m. All I could do was hope that the media would not pick up on it so that we could limit the damage to our remaining dealerships. All our banks were watching our every move. There was nowhere to hide. We could borrow no more money so this liquidation would mean do or die for 2010.

January 2010 came and after a good start to the year for sales we published our ads announcing the liquidations. There was no reaction – initially. But the ads caught the attention of the *Irish Independent* and they ran a fairly detailed story on how we had liquidated two companies. The paper used the Renault logo and the logo of our dealership in Kilkenny. Jesus, this was a disaster. Customers assumed it was all over for the Mordaunts, and sales that had been made for the new year were being cancelled. Not surprisingly the staff were anxious and upset, anyone who we owed money to or soon would came calling, distributors and banks got nervous and Renault were not at all happy to see their logo appearing in the national press associated with a liquidation. It was worse than I had ever imagined it could be.

From the national press the local press picked up the story and ran with it. Renault were not impressed and I was summoned to a meeting with them in late January. We arranged to meet the day after the liquidation, on 29 January, and as the Renault offices were close to Dublin airport I decided to have a weekend away with Anne in Prague and attend the meeting before we flew out. The next major blow was only around the corner. I never saw it coming.

At the meeting I was told that Renault did not see any synergy between our two companies in the future. I was furious and a heated exchange took place between me and five senior managers. I had been completely blindsided. Yes, I had closed a dealership, liquidated two companies and our performance with Renault product in 2009 wasn't great due to the collapse of the Irish economy, but on the other hand I had spent €6 million on developing green-field sites to their specified criteria over the previous five years. I had signed a contract in 2004 that was supposed to signal the start of a long relationship. But car volume sales all over Europe were in free fall. Whether a dealer was twenty years in business, a brand-new dealer or a dealer like me who had nailed their colours to the mast by writing the cheque to build the glass palace, it made no difference. *C'est tout.* Game over.

I flew to Prague a few hours later and spent most of the weekend in bed with the flu. It was devastating news. After another meeting on my return from Prague it became clear that the franchise would be gone within months. Our business plan and forecasts for 2010 were all about Renault. The franchise was set to rocket in market share – and it did in 2010. We had built our entire strategy for the year around their projections. What about all the customers who had purchased new Renault cars from us? What would they think – here today, gone tomorrow. It made us look so unprofessional. It was only 7 February, one week after the liquidations and six weeks into the year. Only seven weeks after drawing down the newly approved funds from the bank. What else could go wrong? It seemed at that point like we were simply staggering from one disaster to another. I closed our Renault operation in Clonmel in March 2010.

Even with the expected increase in market share with Renault, our future in early 2010 was far from certain, despite the positives on the horizon with the new scrappage and VAT schemes. We needed to overcome the publicity of the double liquidation, we had significant creditors to deal with, a mountain of debt that needed to be serviced and some very hostile banks watching our every move. After losing the Renault franchise on top of all this, we now had three empty buildings all with heavy mortgages, and our biggest problem was back to cash flow again, and the effort to try to replace the funds that would have been generated by our Renault offering. Something had to be done to replace it, so I stepped up a gear with my efforts in the UK. I felt that if we moved quickly enough we could capitalise on the seeds we had sown developing an import business. If we could communicate to potential buyers that we could source any used car that they required, we could develop a very sound business that wouldn't eat cash. We invested time and money researching and perfecting the model and finally something went our way. It seemed that the time was right for this. Virtual car sales. It was a brand-new concept and would start us down the road to recovery.

Chapter 10

How the Mighty Have Fallen

Fuck the begrudgers.

Billy Connolly

I knew that once we started closing dealerships there would be a negative effect on both the business and on our family. I worried about the impact it would have on our main dealership, how creditors would react, how it could affect staff, what our friends would think and of course how it would affect my kids. My ascent over the years had been very public, very glossy, very positive. Failure in anything can invoke powerful emotion and, as Ireland has seen over the last few years, some very negative emotion. Regardless of the impact it would inevitably have, the decision to shut down those dealerships had to be taken. For months I had known that the ultimate decision needed to be made – either gamble and hope that I could hang on to everything but at the same time run the risk of losing everything, or take decisive action to protect what we had started out with. This had started out as a family business, built up over twenty-five years, so not resorting to desperate measures to save it was never an option.

Making the decision required all my resolve and determination and I needed to plan how I would manage it publicly. The rumour mill was in overdrive and I needed to exercise damage limitation. We heard the rumours ourselves – in small-town Ireland it's unavoidable. Apparently we were only months from closing the main dealership because we had tax problems. That rumour spread like wildfire, to the extent that my bank manager phoned me to say that I might need to do something or the damage to our reputation would be irreparable. That same day I received another call from someone even more senior in the bank to say that the rumour had spread to Cork and Dublin!

Desperate times call for desperate measures. I had to kill this rumour and jump-start sales. I arranged a live studio interview on local radio which we followed up with a press release, challenging the rumours head on. It worked and instantly the talk changed to, 'Did ye hear about the radio interview that George Mordaunt had to do?' Within two weeks the rumour had died, but I knew that the next six months' trading, when we would be down to just one dealership without Renault, had the potential to wreak havoc on the business, so we needed to prepare.

The ancient Greeks had a battle method called 'burn the boats'. When their armies travelled across the sea to do battle the first thing they did when they landed was burn their boats. With no way to get home unless victory was achieved it strengthened the resolve of the soldiers in battle. I had mentally prepared myself for the post-liquidation battle with the same intensity. Our ability to communicate with the general public and existing customers was going to be tested like never before. Over the next six months everything that could become public knowledge did so and we very quickly learned who our real friends were. Credit accounts we had held for twenty years at the main dealership were closed, suppliers wanted payment immediately, irrespective of whether or not that account was due for payment. Customers who had paid deposits called looking to cancel their deals, and in deals that were being actively negotiated customers would not pay deposits fearing that they would lose them. The forecourt and phone fell quiet, other than those who came looking for money, and then the vultures began to circle, offering thousands below the asking price for used cars, assuming that we needed the cash. With the exception of two or three fellow dealers, the support from the trade itself was very disappointing.

As expected, the rumour mill created all sorts of trouble for us with everyone from the banks to the taxman. I heard one rumour that my wife had run away with a foreign doctor and that I was selling up and moving away. In the thick of it all I was sitting in a doctor's surgery waiting for my appointment when an elderly gentleman in the waiting room started talking about the economy, saying that doctors were recession-proof and would never suffer any financial loss, only to then move on to the subject of cars. He turned to me and said, 'Did ya see that Mordaunt's are gone bust?' He then went on to tell me that the Mordaunts had borrowed €16 million and that the two brothers had fecked off with the money to live in Prague! Seconds later my name was announced on the intercom as I was called for my appointment. As I stood up to walk out I looked back at the gobsmacked man and said, 'Just getting a check-up before I head for Prague.'

People seemed to thrive on our perceived misfortune, loving a good story of failure. I and only I, with no pressure from banks or the taxman, took the very tough decision to close the dealerships as part of a planned programme for survival, but I had experienced first-hand the devastating effects of rumour on reputations and business. In an effort to offset the damage we wrote to our entire customer base explaining that the model on which we had built the motor group was based on volume and as it was very clear that volumes were now gone from the industry we were doing the responsible thing in addressing the problem. We reminded people that it was business as usual. I recorded a number of radio ads offering consumers terrific value on particular cars and quickly discovered that there's nothing like a bargain to get people to forget about rumours. We also created a very strong print ad showing a night-time shot of our magnificent motor dealership and reminding people that we were the longest-serving motor dealership in Clonmel, now in our twenty-ninth year.

Over a period of three or four months the pressure began to ebb away. We had succeeded in overcoming an obstacle so huge it had the potential to shut down our business in one fell swoop, despite having weathered the storm since 2008. Closing the dealerships was painful for me personally, although I tried desperately to convince people that it didn't bother me. I still look at the buildings lying idle with weeds growing around the forecourts and instantly flash back to our gala openings. I often come across photos of the dealerships that we used in advertising and it still stings when I see all the used cars parked around the forecourt. It reminds me of the good times. An abandoned building represents the ultimate failure for me. It is a constant reminder to every person who passes by that we failed. Unless we find a tenant or sell the building it will remain that way. It is very difficult for Anne and the rest of the family to pass those buildings, too. There is real pain among the self-employed when a business fails and it is even more difficult to bear when you hear whisperings of 'Oh, how the mighty have fallen.'

My story of the recession has been all about fighting, holding on and never giving up. But I believe that sometimes the right course of action could be to give up. Give up so that you can start again or because you need to protect what is really important to you, like your family or health. It has become increasingly clear in recent years that all sorts of business models can change. Nothing lasts forever, change is inevitable, especially when the goalposts shift as hugely as they did in Ireland. The economic crisis that occurred in Ireland in 2008 has been in a constant state of flux since it began. It has been my experience that 2011 has been a far more difficult year for trade than 2010, yet in 2009 the predictions were that a national economic recovery would be well underway by 2011, assuming that the necessary corrections would have taken place in our banking system. Yet three years have passed and there is no recovery in sight for small business that I can see.

The Confederation of British Industry (CBI) has said that the recession and credit crunch have become the catalyst for new models in business and a new era that will last for at least a decade. The CBI claims that business owners and their workforce will need to become much more flexible and move to a far leaner model.[16] The longer that national debate about bailouts and bondholders rolls on, the longer we park our opportunity to start on the road to national recovery. One of the biggest issues for small business in Ireland today is not

---

16 www.cbi.org.uk/ndbs/press.nsf/awprdate?OpenView&Start=1&Count=30 allows access to CBI press releases for 2011.

the recession itself but the reaction of the self-employed to the recession. The same can be said about the country – the longer we remain obsessed with the bailout and bondholders, the more difficult and slower our recovery will be.

Our business model for selling cars in Clonmel was built for volume sales. Clearly, any return to decent volume sales is years away, so I have asked myself whether I want to continue with this model until such time as we see a recovery evolving and a sustainable profit being generated. After all, we are in business to make money not just to tread water and earn a salary. Treading water for survival is fine for a period of time, but if that's all you're doing you have to consider how long you think it will be before you see profits being generated by your business again. If you believe that your business cannot achieve profit in future years you must ask yourself the question, 'Should I close?' Borrowing to tide you over should be a one-time-only solution. After that you must trade your way back to profit, and if you can't a tough decision should be made.

Closing is a last resort and might seem radical and result in enormous personal and financial cost, but the scary truth that business owners must confront is that the economy is so badly damaged and there has been such a change in consumer behaviour that it may be impossible for some businesses to recover at all. Rely on your gut feeling and your own experience, not on external advice or speculation. Ask yourself, 'Can I take my talent or area of expertise and utilise it in a business model that will take me out of "treading water to survive" mode and catapult my business to the other extreme where I can make some money?' Question all the 'givens' in your business. Do you need the same-size shop, the same-size showroom, the same number of staff – can you change their roles? Do you need to open seven days a week or would three days be more productive or more profitable? Can you move your business online and eliminate the cost of premises completely? Can you partner with a competitor or a complementary business to consolidate under one roof and share the cost?

This may seem like radical thinking, but this is the kind of thing that businesses are doing to try to survive and make some money again. I did this kind of analysis and it was incredibly helpful – it certainly focuses the mind. Seventy per cent of our sales of used cars since early 2010 have been generated from online enquiries, which means that only 30 per cent of sales come from people walking into the showroom. For us to offer that showroom facility to achieve 30 per cent of our sales I must pay the thirteen staff required to run that showroom and all the overheads that go with it. So sometime in the future I may have to ask, 'Can I make money on total sales at the level that is currently 70 per cent of my business, or even 50 per cent, if I closed the building and let all our staff go, and could I achieve any kind of rental income for the building?' I'd be left with some form of rental income, just two staff (myself and my brother), resulting in a lighter workload, no cash-flow headaches and a healthy business selling used cars online without tying up cash in stock. The margin generated per unit sold versus the margin per unit currently held would be dramatically different. I could make much more money relatively quickly. I could use my twenty-five years' experience, remove all the trimmings and trappings and make a decent living for myself – quite a turnaround from the glory days of 2007 when we offered the people of Kilkenny free helicopter rides when we launched there. Now I realise that I don't need the fluff. I must create my own future because I refuse to tread water waiting for a recovery that might never arrive.

Ireland is sick but it's not dead. I believe that its citizens will get up and go to work every day, pay the taxes and levies, take the hit on the bailout, work hard for their children's future, and slowly, over the next ten years, the country will heal itself. The businesses that will survive are the ones that accept that the economic landscape is beyond recession and can or have reshaped their business model into something that is sustainable without huge volume. There will have to be an acceptance of failure and a change in attitude about it – failure is only for the brave and they should be encouraged to try again, become an employer again, not be vilified because it all went wrong. The economic, political and social landscape has changed and if you have not identified what it is that you are going to do so that your business will cope with doing business and making money in Ireland now, then I believe that you will face a terrible struggle both personally and in business. America and Europe suffered a severe recession. Ireland suffered an economic tsunami. If you changed your business model to adjust for a recession then you have probably discovered by now that you got it wrong.

Chapter 11

Hard Lessons Learned

Experience is a hard teacher because she gives the test first, the lesson afterward.

Vernon Law

Having come through the economic tsunami I have considered what I got wrong and what I would change if I had the opportunity to go back or when the time is right to rebuild, if ever. Our decline was fast and early on in the crisis, but there may be many businesses that are only really beginning to suffer now, and the hard lessons I learned may be of some use to them, so I have listed them here in descending order of importance.

10. I trusted the 'regulated' Irish financial system.

The Irish government from 1999 to 2008 did not regulate the financial-services sector in any way and allowed the country to rely on an overheated property market. They tried to cover up the banking crisis or at least delayed telling the Irish people about it as soon as they knew, allowing us to continue speculating and expanding in a false economy.

Lesson: Plan for only twelve months at any time and trust your gut feeling. Take all the information you can get from financial advisers but trust only in yourself and make your own decisions.

9. I signed agreements without scrutinising them, assuming that I would never need to break the contract.

It's easy to sign contracts when times are good but always ensure you know how you can get out of any contract before you sign it.

Lesson: Sign contracts only when you are absolutely sure your rights are protected and you know how to break the contract. Never assume that you'll be safe to sign based on your relationship with the company offering you the contract.

8. I did not control my stock. Stock control is critical. More stock equals less cash. I didn't have a stock write-down policy.

Instead I followed the route of chasing volume. I pursued market share and not profit.

Lesson: Introduce a strict stock-management programme that includes a write-down policy. Buy more efficiently and protect margin.

7. I did not have the required information to hand quickly enough to make important decisions.

I didn't have the information I needed to make informed decisions soon enough. Accurate monthly management accounts are absolutely vital and you **must** learn how to read them and what the warning signs are so that you can react quickly.

Lesson: Introduce a timely, accurate reporting system and allow time every month to analyse the financial performance of the business using your management accounts – these are your flashlight in the fog.

6.   My relationship with employees became 'too cosy' so became difficult to manage.

I got too close to some of our staff. I often socialised with them and became very friendly with some. This can create all sorts of problems when tough times come.

Lesson: Don't hire friends or friends of friends or friends of employees. Hire based on experience and ability. Show courtesy but keep it purely professional with staff – your private life is yours and theirs is theirs. They will also appreciate this. Be tough but fair.

5.   Not controlling my ego. Thinking I had all the answers and believing my own publicity.

Confidence and ego must be kept separate at all times. There should be no place for yes-men in your organisation. I got too big for my boots and believed that there was nothing I could not achieve, no problem I couldn't fix with flashy marketing and determination.

Lesson: No matter how well you are doing when the good times roll, keep your feet on the ground. Control the powerful desire to do more, buy more and reach that target whatever the cost. Understand that everything should be based on relative profitability. Everything should be stress-tested.

4. Losing the concept of value and therefore ignoring waste.

I didn't measure value for money and believed that our business was bigger than it actually was. Cars, holidays, bonuses and much more became the norm and I took it all for granted.

Lesson: Always spend money only on absolute essentials and become fanatical about controlling your costs. Run both your business and personal expenditure as if every day is in a deep recession.

3. Giving away too much control, not trusting myself.

I stopped trusting my own instincts and abdicated responsibility to managers, accountants and other 'experts'. You are the expert on your own business. Listen to other perspectives but be the boss and own your decisions.

Lesson: If you are feeling uncertain, hit the pause button rather than delegating the decision. Consider, reflect, get all the information and seek some advice, but in the end be decisive and retain control of the decision-making process.

2. Signing personal guarantees to fund an expansion that was way too fast.

I believed the hype that was coming from everywhere, that Ireland's economy was strong and that the worst that might happen was a soft landing, so I thought I was invincible. I borrowed 100 per cent and never said no if I was offered even more. I became greedy and egotistical when it became so easy to borrow money, convincing myself it was because I was such a safe bet rather than because the banks had targets to reach. So I signed personal guarantees which now haunt me.

Lesson: Never ever allow yourself to be exposed personally when financing a business – walk away before you do that. If your business is working and profitable be happy with that and perfect it until you can afford a controlled expansion by borrowing 40 per cent and paying 60 per cent up front.

1. Delegating the most important task in my business.

I stopped doing what I was best at: buying and selling cars. I became a manager and could have hired in that expertise but couldn't replace my own knowledge of business on the forecourt. I removed myself from the frontline where my customers were.

Lesson: Stick to doing what you know best and what is core to your business. Protect your profit. Remain at the heart of your business, making money.

This last point, I believe, was my single biggest mistake, even more so than expanding so quickly. If I had controlled our buying and selling I would have made damn sure that we generated profit on every sale and we would at least have had a fighting chance then, despite the VRT changes and the global downturn.

The most valuable lesson I learned was never to remove yourself from your core business, the activity that really makes money in your company, and do not detach yourself from your customers. When my company grew I assumed that I should remove myself to a higher position, like putting myself in an ivory tower, rather than pushing metal on the forecourt. But the likelihood is that your business grew because you were so good at what you did, so why would you stop doing it? Get somebody else to be the financial controller or office manager or whatever you need. But a word of caution: don't authorise anyone to have sole responsibility for signing anything on behalf of your company and make sure that every cheque written has your signature on it, too.

It is vitally important to never stop doing what got you to the point where you have the opportunity to expand. Recently I visited a big motor dealership in Scotland called Eastern Western Motor Group, which has been in business for seventy-four years. It was established in 1927 and has seventeen franchises. I was sitting in one of their newest showrooms, BMW in Edinburgh. When I asked the dealer principal what makes the group so successful he said, 'We continue to the basic jobs very well, every day of every week.' That's the key. It's so simple really. Your business is your responsibility. Do not depend on others to run it for you. I learned that lesson the hard way.

Chapter 12

The 5 Cs
– These Could Rescue
Your Business

You don't drown by falling in the water; you drown by staying there.

Edwin Louis Cole

Many companies are struggling not only because of the recession but because of the reaction of the business owner to it. Recession causes widespread havoc but, leaving the banks to one side for a moment, I think that the reaction of many business people to the recession has delayed or stalled the economy. It might be hard to believe if yours is one of the businesses suffering, but many companies in Ireland are growing year on year. Some businesses continue to make a lot of money. Some took a hit over the last two years, took it on the chin, regrouped, picked themselves up and moved on. However, there are many companies that took the hit but have not recovered at all. In fact, they don't know how to recover. There is no manual on what you should do and there's certainly no quick-fix guide for mending shattered confidence. It is incredibly difficult for the self-employed to deal with banks and toxic debt, never mind fighting their own demons regarding their ability, failure and starting over. I believe that the problem of the reaction of business owners to the economic collapse has the potential to destroy very functional and potentially profitable businesses that could create employment.

Recovery requires more than just cutting overheads, more than seeking a rent reduction and more than pleading with your bank manager. Business has changed because the spending habits and lifestyles of Irish consumers has changed. If you are a business owner you need to spend less running your company and you have probably let up to 60 per cent of your staff go which will have had an effect on your business – otherwise you didn't need those staff in the first place. Your customers want to spend less, less frequently, than they did in the past. You have (hopefully) less stock and fewer sales, therefore your bank account has less cash, which means that your cash flow will in turn ramp up extra pressure which will ultimately demotivate you and keep you from having a positive 'can do' mentality. How do you stop the rot? How do you turn it around? Where do you go for help? How do you attack the problem, can you afford to attack it and will it be successful? You are not alone in asking these questions.

Whatever your business is, one thing is certain – you are not running it the same way you did four years ago. You may be paying fewer staff smaller salaries, paying less rent, switching more lights off, spending less on advertising, doing no sponsorship, interacting with your bank differently, and managing your cash flow, creditors and suppliers in a completely different way. Your entire outlook has probably, and should have, changed. Assuming that all of those things are already happening in your business, you now need to kick-start your recovery. Your cost base needs to be adjusted to a level that allows your new, but very reduced turnover, to generate a profit. Many companies started to see a decline in turnover in 2008, and three years on, for many, turnover has plummeted despite the hope that 2011 would see an improvement or at the very least a stabilisation. Activity in the motor industry thanks to the scrappage scheme during 2010 helped to boost overall retail sales figures. The feeling within the trade was that this was one of the reasons the government extended the scheme.

Running a company and driving it on are two different things. I think that in Ireland now more effort and time goes into cutting cost than stimulating new business. Cash can disappear for many reasons that you cannot control, but the one thing that you can control is you. Are you obsessed with the recession and the collapse of sales so much that you are no longer driving your company? You may be still running and controlling your business but are you its life and soul? Are you the beating heart, full of life, energy and ideas, or are you the anchor, that heavy deadweight that is holding it back?

I suspect that, like me at my lowest point, many people have lost the will to be the beating heart of their business as a result of what has happened to it since 2008. Fear has gripped so many of the self-employed, fear of closure, fear of failure, fear of what will happen to them if they have nowhere to turn for financial support. Fear that is so awful and obsessive that they forget about their responsibility to their business, so nobody is left driving it. Customers are going elsewhere, the service just isn't what it used to be, the product or range isn't as good as it was, it's available on the Internet €50 cheaper, staff morale is at an all-time low and remaining customers sense that and drift away. The owner doesn't even notice all this because they are self-flagellating while turnover continues to slide, and as a result they are not functioning, not reacting. All the cost-cutting in the world will be irrelevant if you do not do business. You can go out and borrow €100,000 tomorrow and that will remove the immediate threat of fear and closure, and with your new cost base it still won't do anything for long-term stability unless you stimulate customers, sell and retain a margin.

I have seen first-hand many a decent business that could have recovered going to the wall, dying a slow death, and as it dies hearing blame apportioned. Blame the government for not leading/regulating/preventing, blame the bank for not lending or blame consumers for not spending. Instead of playing the blame game I had to take a good long look at myself and my behaviour and I learned that while those were certainly all factors they were not the real reason my business got into trouble. That was all down to me.

So consider this if you are a business owner going through the wars: is it you? Has your business slipped that far because you took your eye off the ball while you were distracted with cash-flow problems and fear? Are you the problem or at least part of it? You became self-employed because at some point you had the metal, the energy, the vision and confidence to start your business, and when you first started you did wonderful marketing, offered great prices, did lots of research, controlled and drove your business. You still should, and if you don't that's the first thing you should try to change. Identify the top-five things you did when you started or took over your business. Here are mine:

1. I controlled everything. Buying, pricing, merchandising, selling. I opened up every day and I closed up. I hired the staff and trained them.

2. I interacted with my customers. I was the face of my company.

3. I signed every cheque, allowed nobody to spend a penny without my say-so and if I could find a way to not spend money I found it.

4. I advertised, watched my competition, aspired to be better, and my ego played a huge role in helping me to achieve my goals.

5. I convinced my banks that me and my ideas were good enough to back. I oozed confidence and positivity. I was hungry, always looking to buy better or sell more.

Success followed the hard work, drive and ambition, so over a period of time I became complacent. Here are the top five things I stopped doing during the boom:

1. I detached myself from the daily grind and created the need for a buffer between myself and my customers, staff and core business.

2. I lost my business focus because I wasn't on the ground anymore and lost my visibility with customers.

3. I became lax in my management style, not running a tight ship and rewarding average performance rather than outstanding performance.

4. I didn't need to talk to my banks because cash flow was not a big problem. I became overconfident and took things for granted.

5. I allowed overheads to climb, paid myself a handsome salary and gave myself a new car through the company. Instead of making money I accepted break-even because I had a decent salary and a nice car out of it. I became complacent.

Once the initial crisis passed and I realised that our business would never be the same again I should have immediately and urgently gone back to behaving as I had done when I started, but instead the fear kicked in, my energy disappeared and I lost all my positivity. Here's how I reacted:

1. I cut costs, stopped paying creditors and allowed bills to mount up. My rent payments went into arrears, I owed VAT and PRSI to Revenue and wasn't proactive with them. My supply chain was threatened until I could clear what was owed.

2. I was so stressed that I simply could not deal with my customers on a one-to-one basis, actually dreaded going to work and was so emotionally destroyed that I couldn't even look at the bank balance. Many people have arrived at the point where they can't even open the post.

3. I started shifting stock at big losses just to get my hands on cash.

4. I was waiting for things to pick up a little. If this is you now, forget it, it is a decade away.

5. I had zero confidence in myself, and my staff, customers, bank manager and suppliers could see it. This certainly wasn't helping my business.

This reaction became my normality until I was jolted out of it and I was lucky to receive that jolt. Many people have not and are still stuck in that hell and so cannot get on to the road to recovery.

Imagine you run a business in a coastal town in Florida, say a small guesthouse or restaurant. You've been in business for twenty-five years and all is well. You make a very comfortable living and have a brisk trade. You lock up one evening, same as you've done for twenty-five years, and head home, go to bed. The next day you flick on the television to discover that the biggest man-made disaster in history has just hit your town.[17] You don't get to open for business the next day. It's over, just like that, in a matter of hours. Gone. No income, no future, no customers, no way around it. That's a crisis – albeit with different challenges. The speed and impact of the disaster are overwhelming and no matter what you do or how positive you are, you are but a very small cog in a very big machine. How would you react? I believe that the fundamental difference between an Irish businessperson consumed with our economic collapse and an American businessperson knee deep in oil is attitude. In America there seems to be a 'we will prevail' attitude whereas we Irish seem to go to ground, see only the negative, become reactive rather than proactive. We blame, we get angry and we get depressed. We are not resilient. As a nation we take the glass-half-empty view.

---

17 In April 2010 a BP oil rig exploded in the Gulf of Mexico, killing eleven people and spilling 206 million gallons of oil into the ocean before it was capped three months later. It was the worst offshore oil spill in American history.

There is still money in Ireland. People are definitely more conscious of value for money but they will spend when they see value. Every day, people travel from all over the country to purchase cars from us, but they do so only because we ensure that every week we are in the top ten cheapest online. We control that and we are proactive about it. Here's another positive; there are over 3.5 million people over the age of fifteen in this country, and a working population of over 1.7 million. That is still a very healthy workforce. Personally, I take comfort from the statistic that there are over two million cars on the road in Ireland today. They all will need to be serviced, they will need tyres and eventually they will need to be replaced, so I must ensure that I am well positioned to take advantage of that statistic.

It is important to brief yourself on the facts and then adjust. My adjustment took place over a three-year period and it should have happened faster, but I was stuck in the hell of fear and inaction. When I finally pulled myself out of that here's a summary of what I needed to do to start a recovery in my business, and these can be applied to all businesses. I call these the 5 Cs:

1. Cope
2. Cut
3. Confidence
4. Creativity
5. Control

Cope

You have to be able to cope with whatever crisis presents itself, in life or in business. Failure to cope can be fatal. Coping skills can be learned. The mind is powerful and can be dangerous if it can't be controlled. In 'the current climate' you may need to cope with challenges that are physical, financial or emotional. To cope with any of these you must identify what it is that's making you feel like giving up. It could be losses, reduction in turnover, collapse in sales followed by the inevitable collapse in cash flow, damage to personal relationships, damage to health, anything.

At first I couldn't cope with the financial pressure but I learned. I chose to cope because I refused to allow my wife and kids to suffer the potential consequences if I didn't. What worked for me was to leave everybody and everything for twenty-four hours and dig deep into my thoughts to figure out the root of my problem and what I could do to solve it, even if it would take lots of small steps to get to the solution. I'd then write this down as a plan and execute the plan in a very methodical and ruthless (if necessary) fashion. I got in touch with suppliers, banks, Revenue, anyone I owed money to, rather than try to hide from them. If I owed a supplier, say, €25,000, I would write post-dated cheques for what I could afford over a period of say twelve to fifteen months and bring the cheques to the supplier, telling them this is what I can afford but, in the meantime, I will pay cash on delivery starting tomorrow. It is imperative that the supply chain is kept open. If you are in arrears with Revenue, do the same. You will be charged interest. Pay it. If you have an overdraft of €100,000 and you are €99,000 overdrawn tell the bank to change it to a ten-year loan for €120,000 including interest and capital and give you back €20,000 without overdraft so that you can start again.

But before you do any of that, find a person who you trust, somebody who is also running their own business, and go to them and ask them for their opinion on your trading difficulties. Arrange to meet this person some evening when the work day is over, tell them exactly where you are and what you are thinking. You cannot be friends with this person. It has to be a person who feels free enough to offer an honest opinion. You need a second opinion. They might see your problem differently and therefore have the solution. There once was a British shoe company that wanted to open a shoe factory in Africa, so in order to establish if there was a market for their product there they sent two salespeople to Africa to carry out some market research. The first one came back four weeks later and said, 'There is absolutely no market there. Nobody wears shoes.' A week later the second person came back and said, 'There is massive potential there because nobody wears shoes.' Two people can look at a problem and see completely different solutions and opportunities, so don't be afraid to seek some independent advice to help you to cope.

Cut

Cut everything except anything that could damage your customers' perception of your brand. Cancel every direct debit and standing order. Review every bill – phone, electricity, mobiles – contact the provider and try to do better deals. If necessary threaten to move to the competition, and if you have to then do it. Go to your landlord and request a rent reduction. If you have not done this already you are two years behind the times. If you did it two years ago, do it again now as rents have fallen even further – if they say they'll sue, tell them what you can pay and let them decide how to proceed. Review how you buy – shop around, bulk-buy, ask for discounts, review downward your stock levels, dump it if you have to. Assuming you have reduced all salaries already, review them again and see if more needs to be done. If you encounter problems from staff who won't buy into the programme, restructure.

Shop around for the very best offers on consumables. I now buy all my paper for our printers from Lidl. It is cheaper than most of the office suppliers. Block your phones from being able to dial directory enquiries, and block staff mobile phones from being able to dial calls other than local calls. Recently I purchased a used car for a customer from one of the biggest motor groups in the UK, and after I took delivery I had a complaint to make so I asked the manager to call me. I was told that he could not call me back as all of their phone systems were blocked from dialling internationally. This group has over 140 outlets. They were well ahead of me. I had four outlets but I never thought to block employees' phones.

This is the level of intensity that you need to consider when cutting costs. Most people did it with rent and salaries but failed to go deep into the overheads. Every €20 saved weekly turns into almost €1,000 per year – and it changes the culture of an organisation that has grown fat in the good times. Every line of your profit-and-loss account should be scrutinised. I halved my rates payment – didn't ask, just did it. What can the local authority do as long as you are paying something? They can send in the bailiffs but that incurs cost for them so as long as you're paying something it may not be worth their while. Don't ignore the perks – where you can, cut expenses, mileage and company cars. I have told my staff that I will pay for milk and toilet paper for our office but that's it. You must go on the offensive and leave nothing untouched when it comes to making cuts.

Confidence

The future of business is about selling yourself and your business to banks, staff, suppliers and customers. To do that you will need confidence. Bucket loads of it. Not to be confused with ego. Confidence can come from being prepared, having all of the information, a proven track record, the belief or knowledge that you are doing what's best for the business and that it will return to profit once remedial action is taken and you have turned the ship around.

Your body language and the confidence in your voice are so important, especially when it comes to keeping your bank onside. The days of picking up the phone and getting an extension to your overdraft or arranging a term loan are gone. Make an appointment and go to meet with them. Show them you take this seriously and know what you're doing. Have you worked out what it costs to run your business on a monthly basis? Do you know what you need to turn over to break even every month? Your turnover is down 50 per cent so what cuts have you made to survive that drop? What are your profit margins like? Do you *think* you are making 60 per cent gross profit or are you *actually* making it? Ask yourself these questions so that you have the answers and can tell the bank before they ask.

If you cannot answer all of the following questions you are at a huge disadvantage:

1. Do you have accurate management accounts?
2. Are they produced monthly?
3. Have you created budgets and a business plan for the year ahead?
4. Will your management accounts report actual performance versus the budget?
5. Have you created accurate cash-flow projections?
6. Have you got a plan B if your turnover falls even further?

Any meeting with your bank from now on should achieve this objective first – show them that you are confident, well-informed and in control. If you attend a meeting with the bank without a plan, with no accounts and no vision, you will get nowhere. In fact, you will damage your reputation and possibly your business as a result. You must instil utter confidence. If you cannot answer yes to the questions posed above you should think about spending some money and getting this information together as soon as possible. 'Information is the greatest commodity you can buy.'[18] Buy it. It will make you far more confident.

Creativity

The world has changed. Consumers have changed. They have been forced to. Disposable income is a luxury. Offering the best possible price is essential. Having the best presentation or merchandising is essential. You've got to get creative with your marketing and your business model, you have to step it up a gear. It's no longer just about traditional media, it's about social networking and digital media. You need to have an online presence and be up to speed with Facebook, Twitter, Google Adwords. It's all about search engine optimisation, metadata, data collection, texting, emailing, customer loyalty points and keeping one step ahead of your competition.

---

18 Well-known statement by the character Gordon Gekko in the 1987 film *Wall Street*.

In this dreadful economy if you come across a company that is beating the recession there will be three reasons that explain their achievement. These reasons are the same in every company. I have 100 per cent confidence in this. They are:

1. Fantastic merchandising.
2. The company has the 'edge', in that whatever they do they do it really well and they stand out from their competition.
3. Their marketing is creative and constant.

I can't stress how important it is to ensure that your business stands out. Don't allow a bland approach, always look to shake it up and always push yourself to be the best at what you do in your market. Across Ireland the businesses that are achieving decent sales are doing so simply because the owners are brave enough to try something different and have excelled in what they do.[19]

When did you last get out on the road and spend a week looking at your competition? When did you last visit another country to look at new concepts or get new ideas or just to see what's happening in your industry elsewhere? Have you been to China? What's the next big thing in your business

---

19 For examples of this type of creativity check out the following: www. jameswhelanbutchers.com; www.kellys.ie; www.avoca.ie/home. The results speak for themselves.

– are you looking down the road and preparing? Four years ago the hairdressing business was all about colour, today it's all about hair tattoos. If you run a hair salon you should be working on finding out what will replace hair tattoos. If you own a restaurant you should be eating in restaurants across Europe or the States to see if you can bring home even one new idea. You must stand out, you must force your competition to follow you. Test your business/marketing model by watching your competitors or doing business with them as a customer, and ensure that, whatever your industry, you are the first name that comes into the head of a consumer who is about to buy. Be brave and try to introduce new, creative concepts.

Control

Regain control of your company. Get out of your ivory tower and get back on the ground. You must get back to basics. You must interact with your customers. Nobody should be spending your company's money but you. Make your own decisions – get opinions and perspectives but make the decision yourself ultimately. You decide the where, when and how. You are the boss. It is your baby and nobody will do the job as well as you will. You are the engine, the driving force of your business. It is your vision. Everything should be run by you. Identify the number one area that generates the most profit in your company and control it with an iron fist. You can train someone else to manage the paperwork

– you should stick to what it is that generates your profit: if it is food, cook it, if it's clothes, buy them, price them and merchandise them, and if it's cars, buy them, price them and negotiate the deal yourself.

Control is about instruction, setting boundaries and parameters. It is about educating your staff so that they know exactly what the company policy and their role within it is. This allows them to do their job effectively without running every tiny detail past you but know when to come to you. Hypothetically, you could sit in a room with no windows, no table and a chair and nothing else but a phone. All day you could answer questions from your staff, instruct them and make decisions on the big issues and communicate those decisions. You don't physically need to do much more than use your brain and ability to communicate to be in control in some organisations, probably the larger ones. But in a small business you must be authoritative, ensure that your team know who's in charge, who's making the decisions, who's steering the ship, who's in control.

The 5 Cs can all be directly related back to the top five things I did when I started. Everything has changed but really if you started your own business you don't have to do anything you don't already know how to do. But you may have to start again – that's exactly what I had to do with my business.

My core team and I had identified that the next issue that would emerge in our industry would be a shortage of used cars by 2011 or 2012. As a result we decided to ramp up the used-car part of our business and become the market leader in it in our area so that by 2011 or 2012 there would only be one name in the consumer's head who wanted to buy a used car – Mordaunt's. To achieve this goal we would need to be well networked with dealers in the UK. We had hired the consultant to help us with that and we now had solid business relationships all over the UK, which gave us access to 300,000 quality used cars. We were immediately ahead of our competition and started a marketing campaign around the concept of 'You want it, we can get it'.

We surmised that the days of keeping a stock of used cars (also tying up cash) on our forecourt were gone. Cars are a depreciating item. If I buy a used car in March for €15,000 and haven't sold it by August it will have devalued by €1,300. We had learned that you can't plan too far ahead – both 9/11 and the disastrous VRT changes had proved to us that damaging change can be imposed on you overnight and there isn't a damn thing you can do about it other than adapt fast. Nothing is forever and change can happen very quickly. So we knew that keeping used cars in stock was not an option and cash flow was going to be tight while we continued to service our debt as we needed the working capital we had borrowed to run the day-to-day operation.

We started to advertise popular models online, cars that we knew people wanted based on our experience, informing them that we could get them cheaper than the main dealers could. We went to the motor show in Paris and instead of looking at the cars we studied the people who were looking at the cars. We very quickly established what cars European drivers coveted as well as discovering what the up-and-coming hot sellers would be – especially in the areas of electric cars and green engines. We advertised these desirable cars at prices that placed us in the top ten for the cheapest cars in an Internet search – we could do this because of the network we had built up in the UK. We trained our staff on how to pitch this new sales model to customers. We received a reaction to our ad and to being in the top ten online very quickly.

Before we knew it we were doing what our trade had long believed couldn't be done – selling cars to people we never met, over the phone. Customers were actually agreeing deals for cars that they had not even seen. That's quite extraordinary. We could take an enquiry from Galway, explain our sales model with utter sincerity, cutting out the typical salesman bullshit, agree the price, take a substantial deposit and then source the car.

It has been hugely successful. We're back to selling cars, making money, satisfying our customers and giving them an excellent service and we can do it without having to tie up money in stock. Because the model has proved its mettle, we have invested some money and taken the business online. We created a website called www.wesourceNEcar.com, which allows a customer to source their ideal used car. The customer enters their ideal make, model, mileage and colour. They can achieve this within their budget by either increasing the ideal mileage to reduce the price or increasing the spec if they have more money to spend. The car is sourced and delivered within ten days. There are around forty million cars on the road in the UK where we are now very well connected to the dealer network, so we will find that car. We have been able to instil enough confidence in people to make them buy and pay without seeing the product. 'They' said it couldn't be done. It could. It's different and it stands out. I'm delighted with our achievement and it has done wonders for my confidence. Our research paid off, our model is completely different, our price is usually the best, our range is second to none and our customer base is now national rather than regional.

Taking time out to come up with an idea, to be creative, is important. In 2008, in order to utilise an empty premises that I had bought in 2005, I started a second business, a barbershop, in Clonmel. How could I get creative with a barbershop, to make it stand out from the crowd? I took some time, considered a few opinions, studied the competition and came up with three things. Firstly, decide who the target customer is and make sure the physical space appeals to that market. The niche I chose to target was kids and teenagers. This led me to item two: choose a cool name with cool logos so that the presentation or merchandising of the shop sets it apart. Finally, introduce something new to this barbershop that others in the area don't have, that will

attract the target market. In our case we called the barbershop
Get Your Locks Off, filled the shop with plasma screens,
Nintendo DS machines and Xbox consoles, opened a Wii
interactive room, and installed digital radio and satellite
TV. If you are a fifteen-year-old kid who wants a haircut
or a hair tattoo in Clonmel, where else could you go where
you can play Xbox or hang out in the Nintendo Wii room
while you wait? Little kids who are nervous will sit up in the
chairs with a Nintendo DS to keep them occupied while
their hair is being cut. The shop is cool and totally unlike
any other barbershop. Our haircuts are the most expensive in
Clonmel, but the surroundings and quality of the cut means
that people know they are getting value for money and so
they keep coming back. And we run great special offers to
appeal to our demographic, too, like 'Cheap-ass Tuesday' or
'Half-price Hair' days. It is a big success because we strove to
be different from the outset, to stand out to the point where
we couldn't be ignored, and then offered a fantastic service.

The 5 Cs were the steps I followed to turn my business
around but I would add one more in hindsight – Cash.

Cash is King

Despite many Irish people having had the confidence to
start their own business, many of us don't know how to cope
with trading conditions in a recession that is bordering on a
depression. We have never had to navigate our way in such

a difficult trading environment – even the older generation who have been through recession before have not had to handle the level of economic collapse that the country is facing now. For self-employed people there are few if any places that they can get real, tangible advice, suggestions or solutions. At the height of my troubles I trawled the Internet looking for advice and discovered the following are considered to be the most crucial things you can do to stem your cash-flow problems:

1. Invoice more frequently.
2. Offer discounts for early payment.
3. Invoice earlier.
4. Accelerate collection.
5. Triage payments.

Seriously? That must have been written back in 1975! We are way beyond that and were doing it all anyway. Remedial action is needed to protect cash flow. Ruthless, not for the faint-hearted and no doubt upsetting to read if you are a supplier, but necessary. Here's what I did and it may be helpful to you:

1. Utility bills – electricity, gas, phone – they are creditors like any other so pay at least half on each bill but do not pay 100 per cent until your cash is in a better position. This is why you need to cancel all direct debits.

2. Approach your larger creditors and tell them that you want to discuss a bulk settlement. Offer no more than forty cent in the euro at first but allow yourself to be negotiated up to sixty cent in the euro as your final offer. Tell them that if they accept that payment as a one-off settlement, in future you will pay in advance for their services or pay cash on delivery. If they refuse, tell them it's that or nothing, so sue you. If you owe €10k or less it would be prohibitively expensive for them to do this so they will eventually accept your offer of 60 cent in the euro. If you owe substantially more than €10K and it would be worth their while suing you, extend the pay-down period to a term that is manageable – they will still not want to go to court unless absolutely necessary as that is a very costly exercise.

3. Issue post-dated cheques to creditors who are threatening to stop supplying you but whose product or service you can't remain trading without. Do it over the longest possible time period. If I owed somebody €12,000 I would issue post-dated cheques for €1,000 per month but I would pay in advance for future services – that's attractive to the supplier and eases the pain a bit.

4. Pay what you can as regularly as you can to Revenue. Do not ignore them and endeavour to get it all paid, but do not be scared of their letters and factor the interest and penalties you will incur by paying late into your payment schedule. Pay the interest bill that they will issue.

5. Walk away from credit. It makes life much easier and

removes the pressure of people chasing you for money. Pay as you go whenever you can.

6. Do not give credit. Kill it completely for new business. Lose the business before giving credit. Credit should only be offered to people you have a track record with who you know will definitely pay within thirty days. Set strict credit limits.

7. Open a brand-new current account with a new bank and do not sign up for any direct debits. Nothing should leave that account without you signing for it.

8. Maximise your overdraft on your old current account and park it – make no attempt to reduce it unless the bank allows you to capitalise the hard-core overdraft over a ten-year period. In other words, convert it to a loan but ensure the loan amount is for €20k more than the overdraft was so that you can start off your new account with your existing bank in credit. If the bank fails to agree to this, hold back the last two weeks of lodgements before you change banks so that you can lodge directly to a new account with a different bank, starting your position with the new bank in credit.

9. Restructure your agreements to ensure that you are paying the absolute minimum possible on interest, rent and mortgage payments, but always pay something every month. Do not hide. Be proactive but remember that nothing needs to be solved over the course of two years. It might take ten years.

10. Defaulting on certain debt is possible and inevitable. Banks and creditors cannot fight everybody. To pursue you in court is expensive and difficult. Familiarise yourself with the concept of debt forgiveness and/or debt write-down and discuss this with your bank.

The more cash in your bank account, the less pressure and stress you will feel and the better you will perform. The fear eases and your spirits lift. There's nothing like a decent cash reserve to make you feel at ease. Whatever you need to do to keep cash in your account, you must do it. Banks, Revenue, and even your landlord are just like any other creditor – they will have to get in line just like everybody else. Anyone who says that your approach is unacceptable will have to deal with it. So long as you are paying something, there's very little they can do other than incurring the cost of suing you for money you obviously don't have.

The Five Cs saved my business not because taking those actions generated so much profit that we were automatically out of the woods in terms of generating cash and then profit, but because I confronted the issues that were distracting my attention. The focus and drive of the owner is the number one most important ingredient in the recovery of a small or medium-sized business. Without that, recovery will not happen.

Chapter 13

Debt, the National Taboo

The unspoken word never does harm.

Lajos Kossuth

When I was caught up in the eye of the storm, the actions of my financial partners, the banks, increased my stress, fear and panic levels. This took my focus off my business, which resulted in further losses for the company and a bigger problem for all concerned. The banks themselves began panicking. I believe Ireland would have had a different experience of the downturn without the hysteria of the banks in their reactions to business owners who had loans from them. My panic resulted in us selling cars at huge losses just for the sake of a lodgement – that makes absolutely no sense, but the banks were not willing to listen and didn't seem capable of thinking rationally. I didn't have a clue how to handle them but I learned.

Recession is not new. Many recessions have been and gone. This one in Ireland is somewhat different in that we have the additional problem of the liquidity of the banks. Their reaction to that has contributed to the fear that has gripped people in business. Plato said, 'We can forgive a child who is afraid of the dark; the real tragedy of life is when men are afraid of the light.' The fear and resentment of banks in this country is understandable, I think. Not only have we been let down by the institutions themselves and the failure of our government to regulate them, we have had to dig deep to pay for it. When the IMF/EU bailout happened and we lost our economic sovereignty, it called to mind for me people like Michael Collins, Thomas MacDonagh, Harry Boland, Éamon de Valera and their ilk. Men with true grit and great courage and ability. Real leaders. They must turn in their graves when they think of their successors who were charged with looking after this country, their legacy.

The timing is right for a new Irish hero to emerge. I think it will be a person who stands up to the establishment, who puts the needs of the people first and directs the banks to start writing down their loan books. Is NAMA working? Only time will tell, but either way it's the only show in town when it comes to addressing liquidity in Irish banks. Non-performing loans are more than likely going to remain that way in the short to medium term, but where things will get really tricky for both the banks and borrowers is with loans where to date only the interest has been payable and so the debt has been serviced, but when the capital also falls due and the asset is then only worth approximately a third of the original purchase price, the pressure will become unbearable. How long is it feasible to expect anyone to continue servicing loans that are unlikely to ever be fully repaid and that the bank has probably written off a certain percentage of already?

To focus on the SME sector specifically, as that's where I believe the recovery will start, there are so many businesses in Ireland struggling under the burden of funding 'dead property'. It is my view that it is very likely land and property values in Ireland will not recover in my lifetime, so it would seem clear then that the majority of borrowers will never clear their loans, with interest, in full. In the domestic market, variable mortgage interest rates continue to rise, even before the European Central Bank increases rates. Irish banks are increasing the cost of their funds and premiums because they are losing millions on fixed and tracker rates that were established before the economic crisis, combined with the exorbitant cost to Ireland of borrowing on international markets nowadays. In my case they claimed that my borrower profile had changed and their risk was higher, therefore rates on my loans had to increase. If the debt pile of the self-employed in Ireland is not somehow relieved, even in the short to medium term, employment and growth in the country will remain dormant.

We need to debate this at a national level. Debt write-off should not be a taboo subject in recession-hit Ireland as it may be an achievable solution to encourage employment. The self-employed are the only people who can rescue this economy by creating employment, and job creation is route number one to solving our problems, so that we can hold our heads high again, consumer confidence can return and the tax take can increase. The multinationals will play their part in terms of the balance of payments and exports, but will they drive employment in a contracting economy? I believe it is the peripheral industries that support the export trade that will create new jobs, and they will be created by local entrepreneurs who will not be able to get started if they are servicing debt from a business that may have failed during the economic meltdown as a result of servicing unsustainable debt.

To stimulate job creation, both businesses and banks must confront commercial debt and be decisive on how to sort it out – get creative, because the old ways don't work in our new reality. Now that property prices have collapsed, loans have been written back to their post-recession values, as evidenced by NAMA's valuations, and banks have accepted recapitalisation from the Irish public as a result of their write-off policy. Why then does the loan remain as a 100-per-cent collectible by the bank? How can you go to the country for help and still expect companies and individuals to fund the entire loan, including interest? Isn't it time to get real and address that?

Every ordinary worker in receipt of a payslip in 2011 can see what their individual contribution to the effort to salvage this country is. What are the banks doing for the people who bailed them out? Are they assisting or contributing in any way? Reducing interest rates, lending more frequently, taking a long-term view of their clients who are at least trying to sort out their debt, even apologising to those pensioners who are left with nothing as a result of the collapse of their share price due to their mismanagement? A recession does not destroy property values by up to 80 per cent in some cases. That's a collapse, a depression, but it's my personal view that in Ireland it was the residue of corruption, cronyism, a lack of regulation and a lack of leadership. That's why our homes and investments are worth 35 per cent less or why developments are worth 80 per cent less. How can you hold the ordinary person who signed in 'good faith' for that loan solely responsible? Why is it acceptable for the banks to write down the loan value but not pass that back to the borrower?

I accept that people could take an opportunity to gain an advantage during any such process and that would need to be legislated for, but consider the following example. A person has borrowings of €10 million with assets securing the loans now worth no more than €3 million. That person hasn't a chance of paying that loan back, no matter how hard they try or what they do to try to address it, for as long as property values remain as they are. Banks must accept that writing off a percentage of a loan will be necessary in order to secure a potentially lucrative future with a company where they can see that there is a viable business at the core.

Business owners must grab the bull by the horns and actively start that discussion with the bank.

Many of us still treat bankers with the same reverence that our parents gave to the clergy in the 1950s, giving them far more respect than they deserve based on their track record. They want more security, we give it to them, they require a personal guarantee and we sign. We accept every charge on our account, and when we query them we are bamboozled with excuses to the extent that we just let it go for the quiet life. Now that they have our balls in their hand, we say yes sir, no sir, three bags full sir. But they have not taken their share of responsibility for the debt. Remember that and say no. If you can't afford to pay, tell them, make it their problem. If you feel that you will never be able to pay, hand back the keys. That was the deal first day – you get the money, they get the security if you stop paying. Give them the security. It's not your problem that it's worth 50 per cent less than it was when you gave it as security. You must find a route to recovery and to do that you must get past your debt pile if you have one. It is probably not possible to continue to service your debt without stifling your business – it will kill either you or your business. Start the fightback and force the bank to take their share of responsibility for the debt that is ruining you and/or your business. Here are a few pointers to get you started:

1. Review all the paperwork you signed over the last five to six years: any form of contract, lease or sanction

letter. Compare those documents to the most recently compiled ones and spot the difference. Premiums on costs of funds have increased for the banks. Margins have increased because your borrower profile has slipped and they're charging you more.

2. Have a securities expert examine the documentation for all the security that has been given, especially on any personal guarantees that you signed.

3. Have a solicitor or an accountant review the paperwork with the objective of finding a weak point, loophole or a grey area.

4. Understand all aspects of what it is that you signed. If there's anything you don't understand, go and find out about it.

5. Examine any cross-charges over different properties against current values before taking any decisions to sell.

6. Ask the bank what life-assurance policy value is now required to bridge the gap between what you owe them and what they think the 'sell today' value on your assets is. When you receive notification of the level of insurance required, subtract that from your overall exposure and what you will be left with is what the bank has valued your assets at – this happened to me. By doing this you will have figured out what provision the bank has made for you defaulting, which means that now you know the minimum figure they would settle for.

7. Ask intelligent and provocative questions that really make the bank stop and think. You will soon learn that the banks are dysfunctional. I suspect that any sort of reasonable challenge with supporting evidence would give you the upper hand in dealing with them and take the pressure off you.

These are desperate times and your recovery is in your own hands. Many business owners are wishing and hoping for the recession to end, and while they do so are struggling to service a crippling debt that would probably take two lifetimes to work off. That causes horrendous stress to an individual and their cash flow, which inevitably leads to even more pressure from the bank. Banks actively told me to offload property at any reasonable price to reduce what I owed. If you have been advised to do this, ask the question: 'What happens to the element of the debt that is left over?' They will probably answer that it will become long-term unsecured debt. This is bullshit – they should write it off if you sell to raise cash for them on their advice. You must find an angle to release yourself from unsustainable debt. Right now, if you're paying anything, the bank needs you more than you need them. Have you considered changing banks and making your next lodgement to a different bank? Everything you do in your business now must be about recovery and to recover you have to be released from the shackles of debt that you cannot repay during your lifetime. 'Try and fail but don't fail to try' (Stephen Kaggwa).

Recovery in Ireland will come down to two things: exports and creating employment. With exports leading the way at the moment, we need to push on with creating employment, but that will not happen until the people who create employment, the self-employed, can get out from under their crippling debt – maybe as a starting point for a debate at a minimum of 60 per cent of the value of their loan book. I realise and fully accept that this may be a far too simplistic view and that there will be a reaction and emotional response from all parties on this island, but the lack of debate on the issue astounds me. We need to start talking about it and maybe an alternative solution will emerge in the course of the debate, but we MUST actively look for a solution because it's in everybody's interest that we create employment.

The view that anyone in business held in 2009 and 2010 about 2011 being better and heading for a recovery disappeared with the introduction of the Universal Social Charge in January 2011. This charge has devastated many ordinary working households in the country. It has removed disposable income from families. It has had a shocking effect on consumer confidence, further stalling any hope of recovery in 2011. The recovery in the economy could be years away so you have to take matters into your own hands in your business and that means getting your company to a position where it can trade, pay salaries and at the very least break even. Any debt that you have has to come last on the priority list and be viewed in the context of what your company can afford to repay.

It would be ridiculous to trade only to service debt. If your current repayment on any debt is, say, €8,000 monthly and you can comfortably pay that, great, but if you can't and that repayment is causing stress to your cash flow, go to the bank and restructure to reduce it, but only when you have discovered what you can actually pay. Do not just pick a figure. Do the maths. If the bank won't be flexible, move to a bank that will, if you can find one. What can they do as long as you're paying something?

Imagine if every person in debt took this approach with their bank at the same time. The banks would be forced into a position where they would have to do something. Anticipate the fact that the European Central Bank will continue to increase interest rates as European economies come out of recession, which has already started – this will further increase your current repayment so you have to be ready to take this battle on.

Review your long-term debt. What do you absolutely need to pay? What are you currently paying that has the potential to destroy your company? To answer that, identify which loans affect your ability to trade and if you default what are the legal ramifications? Banks cannot sue everybody. Remember your deal with the bank when you borrowed the money – you got the money and they got the security in case it went wrong. It's gone wrong. Honour the deal. Give them the security. Let them pursue you for the balance, if they manage to sell it. It will take time and money and even that just guarantees the outcome. Unsecured rolled-up debt is not the answer. If you and the bank come to the decision that you should release any asset which in turn leaves a residual debt, you should only agree to this if the bank agrees to forgive the residual.

During the boom years, a typical commercial purchase might have been an acre of land – a good site with development potential. The total cost including legal costs and stamp duty was, say, €1 million. The purchaser applies for planning in late 2007. Planning is granted in 2008 but the economy has already ground to a halt. In the meantime the interest on the loan is being serviced but the repayments are increasing and at the same time the individual's business begins to stall. This person now has the following options:

1. Hope that their business can generate enough money to continue to try to pay the interest and the inevitable increases due to interest-rate hikes. The site is now worth no more than €400,000, tops.

2. Pay half of the interest payments, get into arrears and battle with the bank. There's very little the bank can do with the asset and they will not want to repossess as even they cannot sell it.

3. Default, walk away, and hope that the bank will not seek judgement. A lot will depend on the quality of the security and on the individual's ability to pay if the bank pursues them.

4. Seek permission from the bank to sell the site for the maximum that it can get. The bank could agree to this as any cash into Irish banks is a positive at this time. But what will happen with the residual balance? I think that a solution would be for the bank to park it until a decision is taken to write it off. In the meantime the individual would be able to park the repayments.

So where should you start if you need to engage with your bank on the issue of your debt burden? Have your accountant prepare a realistic statement of affairs that lists:

- All your assets
- Their current value
- Your current loan exposure
- Your rental income
- Other income
- Increased repayment anticipated due to increased interest rates over the next twelve months

Banks like to see well-documented proposals being put forward. One of their pet peeves is lack of information or information presented on the back of a cigarette packet. It happens. This document will demonstrate to you and your bank your actual position and in most cases the result will be hugely negative. It will be the starting point of your negotiation with the bank, and assuming that both parties are being realistic a positive outcome might be achievable.

Banks need to correct their balance sheets within a defined period so that's in your favour because the only way that this can happen is either by their loans being paid (which you both know can't happen) or by the bank making a considered decision to forgive or write down the debt.

There is a difference between debt forgiveness and debt write-off. According to one bank that I had discussions with, debt forgiveness in business is where a client actively engages with the bank and can demonstrate on paper that they don't have the wherewithal to meet their obligations. The bank told me that if I was in this situation I would probably be asked to swear an affidavit that I had disclosed all of my assets and income stream and that I was not holding something on the side, like a villa in Spain for my retirement. Debt write-off, on the other hand, is where a client has not demonstrated a willingness to cooperate and is not making a full disclosure of their financial position. According to the same bank, in these cases they will actively and aggressively pursue these clients for judgements not only over indebted assets but against any future income. They will include the family home in their write-off policy. If the bank is willing to engage with somebody to participate in a write-down and if that person is living in a home that the bank feels is unrealistic in size relative to the amount of debt that is under consideration to be written down, they would then require the client to 'trade down'. If the client refuses to cooperate then any potential write-down would be taken off the table. Debt forgiveness is a method that is triggered by way of cooperation between bank and borrower whereas debt write-down is when a bank aggressively pursues the borrower, seeking judgements against properties and future income.

Destroying Irish businesses because of decisions made in good faith five or six years ago is an exercise in futility. We may never see the values of the mid-2000s again, so what are we going to do with all the green-field sites, commercial shops, showrooms, hotels and apartments that were bought and now cannot be paid for? Rather than taking a view that only the greedy self-employed would benefit from debt forgiveness, I would argue that if the banks had been regulated correctly and executed good lending practice rather than propagating cronyism and golden circles, this country could have avoided the property crash that has resulted in massive negative equity in all areas of both commercial and residential property. The problem was caused by the banks so the solution to the problem should come from the banks.

Self-employed business people who had taken risks to grow their businesses, thus creating employment and thereby contributing to the Exchequer in the form of all sorts of taxes, could not control any of it but are saddled with the fallout from it for the rest of their lives in many cases.

I think the time is right for the banks to be brave, to confront their dysfunctional business the way the self-employed have had to confront theirs, and declare that they will accept an agreed percentage write-down on indebted assets. Imagine the positive effect that a brave and solution-focused move like that would have on business, employment and consumer confidence? The end of the economic crisis in Ireland will come when the banks make an historic decision on long-term debt. The longer the banks insist on holding out for 100 per cent of their loan book to be repaid, the longer it will take for this country to recover. Banks are just like any other company and as such should be treated like one. They should be forced to settle and write down, like every other business that was mismanaged had to.

What about homeowners who are in negative equity? It's going to be very difficult for the banks to design a formula to allow debt forgiveness on residential property, although I don't believe that the same write-down in values should happen with residential mortgages because: (a) proportionally, residential property values have not decreased to the same extent as commercial property values; (b) the purchase of a family home is generally for residential use in the long term, rather than for investment; (c) home owners have already been granted a level of protection against the banks.[20] Some element of a write-down could be proposed

---

20 In February 2009 the financial regulator announced a new code of conduct for mortgage arrears. This document was designed to assist borrowers in dealing with arrears on home loans. See www.centralbank.ie/regulation/processes/consumer-protection-code/Documents/Code%20of%20Conduct%20on%20Mortgage%20Arrears.pdf

for houses bought at the inflated prices of the period 2005 to 2008. The value of the gesture could be seen as a win-win for the government, the banks and the economy. It could be something as simple as allowing a write-off of 20 per cent of the value of an existing mortgage up to €350,000 on the assumption that the house was purchased between, say, 2006 and 2009, and, say, 25 per cent on mortgages over €350,000. Imagine what a move like this would do to stimulate the property market.

The days of twenty or thirty-year mortgages are gone. To help hard-pressed mortgage holders, family-cycle mortgages may be a solution where mortgage terms are for forty or fifty years. It might sound outrageous and there are obvious problems with such a simplistic scenario, but we have to get creative to deal with our problems and recover, and we should at the very least be discussing and debating these options.

According to Olivier Blanchard, chief economist with the IMF, on 28 January 2011, it could take up to ten years for some European countries to return to normal economic growth trends and they will face some very tough budgets and austerity measures trying to address their national finances.[21] It seems clear to me, then, that a bank with the foresight to write down unrecoverable loans will be the bank that makes the speediest recovery. Irish commercial property

---

21 www.finfacts.ie/irishfinancenews/Irish_Economy/article_1021507_printer.shtml

declined in value by 2.4 per cent in 2010, a vast improvement on the 23.3 per cent decline in 2009.[22] Residential property values have declined by 38 per cent on average since the peak in 2006.[23] It is obviously going to take years to recover from such declines. It is my view that the Irish banks were one of the root causes of the Irish economy's collapse and they are one of the root causes of our inability to recover. Now that we the people have recapitalised them, they need to get creative and solution-focused in dealing with their loan books to facilitate the nation's recovery. They owe us that.

---

22 www.finfacts.ie/irishfinancenews/article_1021497.shtml

23 www.esri.ie/irish_economy/permanent_tsbesri_house_p/

Chapter 14

Today

Criticism is something that we can avoid easily by saying nothing, doing nothing and being nothing.

Aristotle

'2011 will play a major turning point in your life, dear Scorpio. The year worth remembering for bringing out a 360-degree change in your lifestyle and habit.' My horoscope for the year 2011. I don't live my life by the signs of the zodiac, but when I read that in January it just about summed up how I was feeling at the time. When I turned forty I told my wife that I expected the next decade to be the best of my life. Now more than ever I believe that. Strangely, the trauma of the last three years has had a profoundly positive effect on me even though it has been hugely stressful and very troubling. I feel stronger and wiser and have learned so much. I feel pride, too. Not the pride of the mid-2000s, which was fuelled by ego, but proud of my response to the crisis, for accepting and taking responsibility when I wanted to curl up and have someone else sort it all out. I learned how to cope, how valuable time out to reflect is, and the true meaning of the expression 'the buck stops with me'. So much of what happened was outside my control because of changes on the global and national economic landscape, but there was plenty that was within my control that I didn't act on quickly enough and which ultimately resulted in the closure of our two newest motor dealerships. For me personally it's been an important learning curve to identify those mistakes and ensure I never make them again.

In late 2010 I learned that the National Enterprise Conference for 2010 would be hosted by the Clonmel Chamber of Commerce. I had not planned to attend but having met with the organisers on a different matter I knew that they were delighted with the line-up of speakers, all of whom either had a national media presence or were CEOs of large companies. Yet when I looked at the line-up I couldn't help but notice that none of the speakers would address the hot topic of how bloody miserable or stressful it is to be in business in Ireland at the moment. I remarked on this and said that I felt that the chamber had a responsibility to address this issue and that it would be important to have somebody who was not so well known or high profile to deliver a meaningful, from-the-heart speech on the topic.

No sooner had the words left my lips than I realised I was now going to be asked to do it. I had no speechifying experience, but had to put my money where my mouth was, so I accepted the invitation. I hoped that my story would help other business owners who would be in attendance, who, like me at one time, were stressed out of their minds and didn't know where to turn or how to start their recovery. I know from my own experience that at the peak of my difficulties I would have liked to hear somebody publicly declare that they had struggled, hit rock bottom, persevered and overcome. I hoped that I could inspire people to fight on if they saw at first hand that it was possible and that they were not alone.

Nine months earlier, when I had hit a very low point, I desperately wanted to speak to somebody who didn't work for me and who wasn't related to me or married to me. I was completely indecisive, my mind was all over the place and I was faced with many decisions that had to be grappled with. I wanted to find a business person who had experience of both success and failure under their belt, who could be honest and blunt enough with me to call it as it was. I needed a completely objective opinion. I approached a local businessman who had been very successful. I had known him for twenty-five years, not as a friend but as someone with whom I had done business. Back in 2008 when everything was starting to fall down around me I ran into him and he said, 'You look tired. If you ever want to talk call me and we'll have a coffee.' At the time I found this strange even though I knew he was genuine. He's a very astute person.

Eighteen months later I called him and we arranged to

meet. I didn't hold back, told him everything. That can be a very difficult thing to do. We spoke for two hours. A week later we met again and during that meeting he encouraged me to hang on. The hair on the back of my neck stood up when he said, 'No matter what, you keep the lights on. You never close, you never give up. If they want you out make sure they drag you by the ankles.' His words had a profound effect on me and reinforced my determination to fight back if ever it waned, as much as the shepherd's-pie moment had. His words had been so powerful and inspiring for me that I wanted to pass on the experience. I hoped that at the conference I could trigger similar emotion in others who were struggling as I had. I feel a genuine affinity with any businessperson who is fighting for survival. I would get in my car and drive all night if I thought that anything I've learned could help somebody whose business is in trouble. I feel like we are in the trenches together.

I prepared my thoughts and ideas for the speech and memorised it but never wrote it down because I wanted it to be sincere and from the heart. The day I delivered it, 12 November 2010, there were government ministers, TDs, CEOs of multinationals, but more importantly, many local business owners in the audience. I was nervous – I was about to stand up and very publicly admit that I nearly lost everything, I fucked up and have a long way to go to get back, that I was terrified but I conquered the fear and am slowly finding my way back. I will survive and my business will survive. You're probably feeling the same way. No need to be embarrassed. Let's talk about it. I hoped to inspire one or two people in some small way, but I was completely unprepared for the reaction that followed the speech. There was powerful emotion in the room. The applause was deafening. For the first time in my life I had received a favourable public reaction and it came from my honesty and openness about fear and failure rather than success and achievement. I was flummoxed.

News reporters in the room described the speech and the reaction, and within three days the story of what happened in the room that day was on the front page of every local paper, made it into the national papers, onto national radio and eventually onto national television. For two weeks after the speech my phone never stopped ringing, with calls from all kinds of media but also from business owners from all over the country calling to see if I could give them any advice or if they could have a copy of my speech – I still regret not having written it or recorded it in any way so that I could share it. These calls were from craftsmen to plumbers to farmers, all in the same boat, all feeling despair and all needing a bit of encouragement and guidance. Everywhere I went people came up to me, shook hands and said well done. People who were previously maybe not my greatest fans had the grace to seek me out to offer congratulations.

It had become such a talking point that in December when Anne and the kids and I were at the airport about to go on a family holiday, the security officer in the airport recognised the name on my passport and asked me if I was the car guy who was in the press. When I said yes, he said, 'Well done and the best of luck in the future.' People were wonderful in their support – their goodwill and sincerity really shone through. It was the most rewarding feeling. The most significant outcome for me, though, was that after all the years I had fought my demons regarding what people thought of me, the public perception of the boss's son and the criticism I got when we expanded so aggressively and my downfall thereafter, I finally felt like I had achieved acceptance. My wife, brother and parents and Sarah were in attendance when I made the speech. It was an historic moment for us as a family, too. Anne smiled at me as I left the podium and her smile told me how much I was loved and how proud she was. When I looked at my father I could see he was moved. After twenty-four years of highs and lows in our relationship, with me constantly trying to prove myself, it was like a veil had been lifted. He saw my intelligence, my resolve, my positivity, my ability to communicate and, of course, my humility. That speech was another milestone in the story of my life.

Even on television I was completely open about the despair I had felt and the steps I had taken to recover. I wanted to share my story and try to demonstrate that we are all in this together so there's no point being embarrassed if you are in an ailing business, or ignoring how difficult life is for the self-employed if that isn't your own situation. After the television interview I spoke to a man who told me that he and his wife had been deliberating for a few days about whether or not to take an opportunity that had presented itself for them to expand their business, and that they had turned it down having watched my interview. They realised that the timing wasn't right and that they were happy with the way their business is currently, with no debt. Whether this was the right decision or not ultimately is up to that couple to decide, but if my story has saved them even a day of the kind of mental anguish that I experienced, it's the right choice.

I believe that as a nation we need to address our quality of life as a matter of urgency. The economic crisis has ramped up stress levels in the lives of thousands of families. According to research, behavioural changes can occur in children as a direct result of anxiety caused by financial stress in the home.[24] Children pick up on their parents' worries and many parents are worried that they will not be able to put food on the table. Anecdotal evidence suggests that evictions and repossessions are increasing; depression, marital breakdown and even suicide have blighted the country over the last two years. We can't continue like this. As it is, our children

24 www.suffolk.gov.uk/NR/rdonlyres/320E5D8B-E2DE-49E8-976A-95C87541D97F/0/EffectsoftheRecessionandThosemostatRisk.pdf

will be paying for our mess over the next two decades. We have a moral responsibility to protect them from the toxic economy that we will pass on to them. In the summer of 2010 there was no mention of the IMF or Ireland receiving a bailout from Europe. Within six months the news broke, the negotiations were complete and the cost was inflicted on the nation in the form of the Universal Social Charge. In six short months any hopes that we privately held about recovery were dashed.

In 2010 the top three countries to live in for the best quality of life were (3) Switzerland, (2) Australia and, (1) (for the fifth year running) France.[25] Ireland lies outside the top forty. There are obvious traits that spring to mind in each of the top three. Switzerland is considered to be well organised, efficient and self-sufficient, Australia has a robust economy, a great climate and an outdoorsy culture, France has a great culture of food, wine, history and a world-class health-care system. Ireland could compete in the areas of food, history, outdoor activity, culture, the arts and, with a concerted effort, economy and a health service. But we are still outside the top forty. How much further will we slip given our austerity package and dependence on the IMF/EU?

Our economy is still uncompetitive. For example, in the UK the standard flu vaccination is administrated for

---

25 http://top10hell.com/10-best-countries-to-live-in-2010/

£9 while in Ireland it is administered at a cost of €38.95.[26] According to the National Competitiveness Council Irish medical consultants are the highest paid in the OECD countries, earning almost double that of their equivalents in Finland and Norway. A firm specialising in insolvency quoted NAMA €800 per hour for an assignment.[27] Our lack of competitiveness must be tackled and we may have a backlash of industrial-relations problems as a result, but it has to be done. If our governments were as ruthless at imposing sanctions on wastage as they are on taxing our people we might just see a more balanced recovery.

Populations apparently get the governments they deserve, but we have limited options. During the election campaigns of 2011 I can't recall any party basing their campaign around improving Irish society. Society and a healthy economy are interdependent and certainly should not be mutually exclusive. National policy can address or at least influence this. Look at how with the introduction of the SSIA scheme the government was able to influence a culture of saving and planning. Our way of life is at stake and we need to become more interested and aggressive in determining our future as a nation. Perhaps we could learn a thing or two

---

26 www.finfacts.ie/irishfinancenews/Irish_2/article_1017954_printer.shtml

27 'Irish General Election 2011: Dublin Chamber calls for "root & branch" public sector reform; Silent on reform of protected private sector', available on www.finfacts.ie/irishfinancenews/Irish_Economy/article_1021550_printer.shtml

from the French. As long as we continue to be number one in the rankings of professional fees and other costs, we will continue to stall our recovery, which could prolong a below-acceptable quality of life. We continue to be a nation of cute hoors, unfortunately. I think that needs to be replaced with a society in which we refuse to accept and actually punish corruption, backed up with a zero-tolerance policy on waste and cronyism.

I still work hard and fight every day to ensure my business's survival and take nothing for granted as the country remains in a perilous economic position. Sales are still very slow, but it seems like the worst may be over – for my business, anyway. It may be only starting for yours. New-car sales are growing slowly and our online services continue to generate reasonable levels of customer enquiries that translate into sales of used cars. We hope to perfect our virtual sales model in the coming years and I still feel a great sense of achievement that we are able to sell a car without a customer even seeing it, let alone test-driving it.

We still own most of our buildings, except the Renault building in Clonmel which I sold. Despite being surrounded by empty buildings I continued to service mortgages on them for as long as I could. Some months full payments, other months half payments. Eventually I decided to take matters into my own hands and decided to use my marketing skills to advertise turnkey rental properties suitable for motor dealers. Many potential tenants wanted to open their own operations but they couldn't afford the kit-out. A turnkey option increased the rent but allowed them to pay monthly as opposed to paying for fitting out the building up front. It was a successful move and in time I sourced tenants for all our buildings. With my drip-feeding of the mortgages and the banks' support I was able to retain full ownership.

I believe that the best years are still to come in my career because of what I have learned over the last three years. I feel triumphant in having survived and remained trading, albeit in a completely different guise, but I accept that I have failed in some areas and take full responsibility for that. I have learned, however, that failure is not as devastating as it sounds and that processing and accepting that failure is not the be all and end all is a skill worth developing. Good things have come from failure. As Walter Brunell said, 'Failure is the tuition we pay for future success.' That could be a slogan to describe Ireland's economy at the moment.

My biggest education in the last three years has been understanding that a failing business is not terminal cancer. It is not a death sentence and if that is the effect it is having on your life or your lifestyle and your family, it is OK to walk away. I missed too many sunny summer evenings, beautiful autumn days and frosty winter mornings with my family. How many funny or tender moments with my kids did I miss while I was consumed with the terrible fear and worries that I had over the last three years? I will never get those days back. I was lucky that my health was not compromised on any serious level, but it could have been. Do not be afraid to walk away if that is the solution. Life is too precious to waste on keeping dysfunctional banks at bay.

When I set out to write this story I wanted to offer real advice, or at least share the benefit of my experience of twenty-five years working in a family business and everything that goes with that, as well as experiencing boom to bust in a broken economy and learning how to cope and emerge relatively unscathed. I hope I have achieved that, and here is a summary of all that learning, in no particular order:

- Try to avoid working with family if you can. It can be rewarding if successful but cruel with devastating consequences if it goes wrong or doesn't work out.

- Ensure you help your kids to discover and follow their talents, and don't invite them to work with you unless you have planned a succession strategy.

- Take a critical view of your business or whatever you're trying to figure out based on the facts, and listen to your gut feeling. Ensure the criticism is delivered professionally and productively.

- Avoid expansion based on an overconfidence or ego. Expand only when you are sure that you can increase your profit, can finance at least 60 per cent of the expansion yourself and can service any remaining debt over a defined time period.

- Expansion should be based on decades and not a three-year plan.
- All borrowing should be at a ratio of 60/40 – borrowing the lesser.
- Trust your team but keep the relationship professional and remain in control even when you delegate.
- Take counsel but in the end make your own decisions.
- Control the heart of your business – the bit that generates the profit.
- Do the basics really, really well.
- Be honest, direct and sincere – no bullshit required.
- Pay what you can, but always pay.
- Seek help if you need it – don't alienate yourself because of pride.
- Produce management accounts monthly.
- Market analysis is crucial.
- Never sign personal guarantees.
- Never cross-secure any loans and always review agreements and contracts with your legal advisor. Know how you can get out before you sign.
- Be creative, stand out from your competition and constantly research.
- Treat the start of every week as if it was your first week in business.

Epilogue

If you want a happy ending, that depends, of course, on where you stop your story.

Orson Welles

Family business, boom to bust, recovery. I told my story and it has changed me, but I feel unsettled, as if I've missed something. It's not that I made mistakes, because I've accepted that, nor is it the state of the Irish economy and the very difficult challenges that lie ahead for all of us. It isn't the injustice and corruption, the pay-offs and pensions, although they are infuriating, and it isn't the fact that we have lost our economic sovereignty. It is how we took it all.

We took it in the guts and didn't even object – collectively, where there's real power. With the exception of that hardy generation who took to the streets when their medical cards were threatened, we have not mobilised as a nation to say we've had enough. I include myself in this collective. We have allowed governments to make a mockery of us because we accept whatever they tell us without reacting, and succumb to their politicking – the IMF are coming, no they're not, yes they are. The banks are fine, no they're not, well they're not as bad as they could be, um, actually they're worse. We sat at home and grumbled and complained to each other but as a nation we took it. We sat there watching the multimillionaire developers and bankers take the piss out of this country with absolutely no consequences because of God knows what loophole, we allowed executives of banks and semi-state bodies that we own to walk off with massive payouts and pensions having played out a real-life game of Monopoly with our money.

Even if we couldn't do anything legally, we could have objected. What is it in our culture or national psyche that is holding us back? Is it apathy or fear? In 2010 one million women took to the streets in Italy to object to their Prime Minister's treatment of women, the Egyptians ended the almost forty-year reign of Mubarak by taking to the streets, and the Libyans are now following a similar path. The Greeks have shown their government what they think of the mismanagement of their economy, but in Ireland we just seem to hang our heads lower. I don't really understand it and can't even explain my own inaction in terms of demonstrating. What created that drive for improving the lot of Irish citizens in men like Wolfe Tone, Robert Emmet and Charles Stewart Parnell, to mention just a few Irish heroes? Why do we lack the urgency and drive to seize control of our own future in this generation? Is it because we're embarrassed, having 'lost the run of ourselves' during the boom years? Or because deep down we really believe that average is the best we can be?

We moan but we do not demand, we begrudge but we do not lead, we allow our politicians to offer empty promises but never hold them accountable.

We have an obligation to future generations to say stop, we have an obligation to improve our society as well as our economy and to start ruling with absolute transparency. All those who are privileged enough to be in a position where they can make a difference, or have been elected to act in the best interests of this country, need to stand up and be counted. This book is my call to action: let's do things differently, let's be more decisive, more ruthless when we need to be. Let's stop accepting and start objecting. Let's think about the next ten years in this country. I want my kids to live in a better Ireland but find myself wondering if they would be better off living and working in a country like France or Switzerland. Each of us has a responsibility to be able to answer to our children when they ask us what we did when the opportunity to change our society arose. A single letter of objection to a TD might make little difference, but if a single letter became over two million letters they would grab some attention.

My life now is all about learning. The older I get the more I understand how little I know. I am happy with less and have learned what really matters to me and take pleasure from that. More than anything, my life now is about never being forced to do something that I really do not want to do. This whole experience has made me tougher, more resilient, and has equipped me to avoid the pitfalls in the future. Les Brown said, 'If you fall, fall on your back. If you can look up, you can get up.' Find your reason to get back up. My reason was the same one that inspired me to share this story: my family, Anne, Emily and George.

I will move forward having learned to keep a firm grip on the massive ego but not giving an inch on the rehabilitation of my business. I believe that the battle for recovery continues and that we are all in it together. When I reflect on this journey and consider the welfare of that old rock in the Atlantic called Ireland, its challenges and the challenges that lie ahead for its people, I think to myself, 'This too shall pass.'

Acknowledgements

I would like to thank some people who have supported me and helped me rediscover my mojo and in doing so helped me find the way forward.

Firstly to so many local Clonmel people and to all Mordaunt customers past and present. Your support will never be taken for granted. Thanks to Tommy and Sean for fixing my head.

Thanks to Winnie and Michael for all their support. To all my past and present staff thank you for your individual input. To all who offered advice along the way, you know who you are, but especially to John Fraher for his personal input.

To Clodagh and all at Mercier Press – truly outstanding.

To my sisters Lizanne and Claire, who didn't feature very heavily in the book but who remain constant in the background. To Sarah, thank you for never giving up. Your unconditional support in good times and bad will never be forgotten. I owe you so much. You remain our greatest-ever employee. To my brother Brian, who will always have the ability to crack me up, I thank you for your absolute love and support and trust. Here's to the next twenty years.

A big thank you to my mother who refereed many an argument over the years, for her one-to-one counsel, for always backing me and for believing that I could turn it all around. Thanks Mam. To my dad, I can only say that despite all our ups and downs I love you, and you will always be the greatest salesman I have ever known. Thank you for teaching me your skill. Thank you for everything.

To my kids Emily and George, I hope you're proud of *Shepherd's Pie*. You inspired it. You started my fightback. You saved me. I could not ask for better kids. I love you.

Finally, a big, big thank you to my wife Anne. Your fearless bravery, your utter trust and faith in me, your advice, your support, your love continue to blow my mind. Thanks babe.

To all the struggling self-employed people around Ireland, I hope this book inspires you to continue fighting. Remember, no matter what keep the lights on.

MERCIER PRESS

IRISH PUBLISHER - IRISH STORY

We hope you enjoyed this book.

Since 1944, Mercier Press has published books that have been critically important to Irish life and culture. Books that dealt with subjects that informed readers about Irish scholars, Irish writers, Irish history and Ireland's rich heritage.

We believe in the importance of providing accessible histories and cultural books for all readers and all who are interested in Irish cultural life.

Our website is the best place to find out more information about Mercier, our books, authors, news and the best deals on a wide variety of books. Mercier tracks the best prices for our books online and we seek to offer the best value to our customers, offering free delivery within Ireland.

Sign up on our website or complete and return the form below to receive updates and special offers.

www.mercierpress.ie
www.facebook.com/mercier.press
www.twitter.com/irishpublisher

Name: _____

Email: _____

Address: _____

Mobile No.: _____

Mercier Press, Unit 3b, Oak House, Bessboro Rd, Blackrock, Cork, Ireland